INCOME AND JOBS: USA

INCOME AND JOBS: USA

Diagnosing the Reality

George Sternlieb
and
James W. Hughes

CENTER FOR URBAN POLICY RESEARCH

Published in the United States of America
by the Center for Urban Policy Research
Building 4051 — Kilmer Campus
New Brunswick, New Jersey 08903

Library of Congress Cataloging in Publication Data

Sternlieb, George.
Income and jobs, USA.

Includes index.
1. Income distribution—United States. 2. Labor supply—United States. I. Hughes, James W. II. Title. III. Title: Income and jobs, U.S.A.
HC110.I5S875 1984 339.2′0973 84-5889
ISBN 0-88285-101-2

Table of Contents

List of Exhibits

Chapter Seven

Chapter Eight

Appendix A

Preface

Panic is a potent child of ignorance and faulty information. In no area is this more evident than the kaleidoscopic changes in perspective on the economic present and future of the United States. Abrupt shifts from ebullience to despair are evidenced not only by the media, but by the public as a whole. We are inundated by a psychological boom and bust cycle, moving with a rapidity which has left analysts and investors staggering in its wake.

Contradictory signals from savants abound. Every newspaper desperately adds staff to its financial section; broadcasting services vie for the services of media economists and crystal ball gazers. The search for newsworthy statements has created an enormous appetite for selective vision, for data sometimes chosen out of context, to prove a priori belief.

The *nominal* facts are increasingly the backbone of the learned and unlearned alike. But the taste for nominally ''hard'' statistics often obscures the fact of how ''soft'' they really are. Assertion and counterassertion, claim and counterclaim, arrive faster than understanding. Whether investor or spender, pro-Administration or anti-, a better grasp of reality is required — Where is America going in the 1980s?

- Are the incomes of Americans declining?
- Is the middle class — and most importantly, the mass middle market — disappearing?
- Has the United States standard of living fallen behind other advanced industrial nations?

- Are we really becoming a nation of low-wage, fast-food attendants?
- Are America's minorities falling off the income train?
- Is poverty soaring to new heights?

Popular media headline accounts view the 1983 recovery as an aberrant, and at first blush, affirm the legitimacy of these questions. A somber appraisal would also result from a superficial scrutiny of income and job statistics.

- Between 1973 and 1982, the median family income of Americans fell from $26,175 to $23,433 (in constant 1982 dollars), a decline of 10.5 percent.
- Between 1973 and 1982, the number of families with incomes between $15,000 and $35,000 (in constant 1982 dollars) — the broadly defined middle class — contracted from 51.3 percent of total families to 44.0 percent. The proportion below $15,000 surged while the share above $35,000 expanded slightly.
- As measured by Gross Domestic Product (GDP) per capita (converted to U.S. dollars via 1975 exchange rates and price levels), income in the United States ($8,078) in 1981 lagged Switzerland ($9,413), Sweden ($9,203), Denmark ($8,365), and Canada ($8,208) — and was at parity with Germany ($8,056).
- The United States lost 1.3 million manufacturing jobs between 1973 and 1982, jobs whose gross weekly earnings averaged $331 in the latter year. Concurrently, services employment exploded; however, gross weekly earnings in this sector averaged only $225. Neither General Motors nor U.S. Steel have as many employees as McDonald's.
- In 1973, black median family incomes were 58 percent of those of white families; by 1982, the ratio had declined to 55 percent. Spanish origin families were also falling behind their white counterparts.
- The poverty rate in America stood at 11.1 percent in 1973, one half the rate of 1960. But by 1982, it had moved sharply upwards to 15.0 percent. The number of persons below the poverty level increased by over 11 million between 1973 and 1982.

The American economy, pounded by an unparalleled series of "shocks" in the 1970s, undeniably stumbled, at least in contrast to the halcyon years of growth and stability in the decades immediately following World War II. But the rest of the industrialized world was not left untouched; it too has been struggling to adapt to the new imperatives that have emerged in the past several years. Evaluating the United States in a vacuum can lead to faulty conclusions.

Moreover, statistical generalizations prove hazardous without awareness of alternative data series, base year selection vagaries (business cycle peak or trough), inflation standardizing limitations, inhibitors to precise international comparisons, and the impact of unique and singular underlying demographic shifts. Alternative visions of reality are intimately shaped by the decisions of those analyzing and presenting the data.

- Inflation adjusted (constant 1982 dollars) personal income per capita grew from $9,795 in 1973 to $11,071 in 1982, a nine-year gain of $1,276 — 13.0 percent — in the average *real* personal income accruing to each American.
- Viewing income distributions from 1975 to 1982 (recession to recession) rather than 1973 to 1982 (business cycle peak to recession) suggests not so much the pulling apart of the middle class, but a thickening-up of the upscale market. The percentage of families with incomes $35,000 and over (in constant 1982 dollars) increased from 22 percent to 27 percent between 1975 and 1982.
- Measuring GDP per capita internationally via Purchasing Power Parities (PPPs) — the internal domestic purchasing power of each local currency — the United States in 1981 far outdistanced most of its other industrial peers. According to this measure of economic well-being, the position of the U.S. has changed minimally over the past decade. Indices of GDP per capita, using current PPPs, show the U.S. in 1981 at 129 percent of that of OECD (Organization for Economic Cooperation and Development). In 1975, the index stood at 131.
- All advanced industrial economies have been losing manufacturing and/or ''smokestack'' jobs. However only the United States has shown an unparalleled competence in generating new jobs — perhaps not all premium ones — but levels of absolute and comparative growth in employment that have no parallel in other developed nations. While the four largest European countries in total had a net *loss* in total civilian employment between 1970 and 1982, the United States economy expanded by almost 21 million jobs, or 26.5 percent.
- Not all black families are experiencing relative income declines. However, profound income-demographic segmentation is underway, a phenomenon obscured by overall median statistics. In 1981, black married couple families with both spouses working full time had incomes almost 90 percent of their white peers. In contrast, black female householder (single spouse) families had median incomes barely 60 percent of those of their white counterparts. Since this demographic configuration dominates black family growth — 42 percent of black families in 1982 were female headed (spouse absent) — internal black income cleavages are widening.
- Poverty rates have increased in the post-1973 period. However, there is a strong cyclical component to poverty trends, which rise and fall in conjunction with the business cycle. In this context, the 1980 to 1982 rolling recession had a major deleterious impact on the statistical portrait. Concurrently, major demographic shifts also underpinned poverty growth, with the surge of female (single spouse) householder families dominating the overall rate increase.

What is reality and what is apparition? Was America irrevocably battered by the stresses of the 1970s and early 1980s, or was it subject to the dislocations of a difficult, but successful, adaptation to a new economic and demographic order? Careful navigation across a very sticky statistical terrain is essential just to begin framing responses to these questions.

THE BROADER OBJECTIVE

In this book, we have attempted to provide a concise overview of the basic data with which to analyze the major income and job trends that have concerned marketers, analysts and policymakers alike. Of particular concern are the perils and pitfalls inherent in the statistical data bases — the confusing and conflicting signals they often evoke — and the potential for resolving what appear to be fundamental discrepancies. As was the case with our predecessor volume (George Sternlieb, James W. Hughes and Connie O. Hughes, *Demographic Trends and Economic Reality: Planning and Markets in the 1980s*), the perspective is that of the planner, concerned with the implications of broad social and economic parameters for public and private decisionmaking and strategy.

In this context, future directions and their consequences are of major import as general guidelines to the task. How should we scrutinize the past in order to secure at least fragile handholds for the future? What are the alternative income and job patterns that emerge from broad data analysis? What are the forces which underlie these patterns and how will they change in the future? Is the present era — the mid-1980s — a temporary plateau, or a springboard to the future?

ORGANIZATION

Each of the broad issues that we have targeted is enmeshed in rich and wide-ranging data bases. Within the framework of our limited objectives, however, it has been necessary to strictly demarcate the bounds of both the subject matter and data resources considered. Indeed, each of our chapters could have been the focus of separate in-depth research monographs. Our goal is to present the fundamental building blocks of income-job data, and to suggest some of their general implications.

The study begins with a broad non-quantitative conceptual overview of the critical economic parameters and contours of the 1970s (and the range of accompanying explanations) and their transformation during the 1980s. To further set the stage for the detailed U.S. statistics, international income comparisons are then undertaken. The major income partitions in the U.S. are subsequently detailed — median family income versus per capita personal income and household versus family income — with particular attention granted to the structure and composition of the two major data bases. Comprehensive family income analyses are then presented, exploring business cycle and demographic linkages. Subsequently, emphasis is directed to the association between the evolving employment structure of the U.S. economy, shifting earnings patterns, demographics, and income. Racial and ethnic variations are then explored, particularly in regard to the demographic underpinnings of observed income differentials. Finally, the caboose of the American economic train — the change in officially defined poverty — is considered in the context of the preceding phenomena. The detailed chapter partitions are as follows:

Chapter 1: The Changing American Context

The critical events and benchmarks (or ''shocks'') that characterized 1970s' America are reviewed, explanations of the resulting performance of the economy considered, and changes in the basic parameters of the 1980s (the new ''fundamentals'') suggested.

Chapter 2: International Income Comparisons

To set the stage for internal examination, the relative income position of the United States in an international framework is undertaken via alternative measurement criteria. The analyses demonstrate the complexity of the basic task, the sensitivity of the results to the assumptions of the analyst, and the superficiality of popular assertions.

Chapter 3: Personal and Family Income: Elation or Despair?

Trendlines and patterns of change in per capita personal income and median family income are established and compared. The strikingly different pictures painted by each of these statistics are reviewed in terms of their underlying data series, inflation correction procedures, and demographic vagaries.

Chapter 4: Household and Family Income

An overview is provided of household income — the broader pool from which family income, as well as a whole variety of marketing and policy generalizations, is drawn. The examinations lend preliminary demographic explanation to the behavior of income trends, and set the stage for more detailed analyses of family income parameters in America.

Chapter 5: Family Income: Post-Affluence or Demographic Distortions?

An extensive detailing of the dynamics and patterns of income growth and change is presented. The major demographic partitions and the influence of business cycle positioning in data interpretation are considered, particularly their impact on the principal statistical indices.

Chapter 6: Employment, Earnings, and Income

Changes in America's employment structure, the variations in earnings across industrial sectors, and the relationship of earnings to income are explored. International comparisons are provided, and the influence of demographics and the business cycle is suggested.

Chapter 7: Racial and Ethnic Income Variations

A continuation of the distributional patterns of income is provided, focusing particularly on black-white and Spanish origin-white income differentials across the array of family configurations.

Chapter 8: Poverty

The basic dimensions of America's poverty population and families are isolated, and the long-term shift in composition examined. Again, particular attention is directed at the major demographic linkages.

Chapter One

THE CHANGING AMERICAN CONTEXT

Economic statistics are not merely passive measuring sticks of things past. They can be highly subjective shapers of our vision of today's reality and thus set the requirements of tomorrow. Once the nearly exclusive terrain of small groups of economists, such indicators as gross national product, labor force participation rates, and the array of income measurements — per capita and median family data, etc. — are all now the stuff of front page news in the daily press. They are targeted by various groups which, consciously or otherwise, select those elements which tend to support their visions of the world. And, much more importantly, the way it should be — and how to get there.

The shocks administered in the past decade to the American sense of well-being, of certainty and destiny within the world economic order, have created an unparalleled hunger for forecasting. But the forecaster's art still depends upon a matrix based on history. What *has happened* — willy-nilly — is still the predominant shaper of our predictions as to what *will happen*. Within this context, the pattern of change of median family income within the United States is suggestive. Its shrinkage (in constant 1982 dollars) from $26,175 in 1973 to $23,433 in 1982 is a significant, but far from extraordinary, measure of the erosion of the foundations of America's economic complacency. And this should be put in the context of the virtual doubling of real incomes which occurred in the generation prior to 1973.

America and Americans traditionally have been the true home and upholders of the theory of progress, of a belief that while there may be brief eruptions in the system, the basic trendline is onwards and upwards. While this concept received serious challenge in the era of the Depression, it was certified by the revolution in standards of living which took place in the relatively unmarred flow of the 25 years following World War II.

The very hegemony of America in the world economy, the simple implicit belief that things are better here than anywhere else, has been denied by observers pointing to the relative income decline of the United States on an international comparative base. For example, by 1981, the per capita income of a number of countries by some accounting standards equalled or surpassed that of the United States.[1] In that year, income in Switzerland was 117 percent of that in America, Sweden's — 114 percent, Denmark's — 104 percent, Canada's — 102 percent, with Germany's at parity — 100 percent. And these are nations which typically had incomes far below their American counterpart a generation ago.

Statistics and data accounts such as those cited have been used by a number of critics of the American economic delivery system. In turn they propound the issues of whether alternative forms of organization, of market and industry targeting, of tax policy and of investment are required lest the United States and its people lose their cutting edge.

Theses without end have been espoused in this regard. For the Marxists, for example, the increasing depth of our domestic economic cycles heralds the ultimate demise of a capitalist system. To others, it is merely an issue of tired blood, i.e., of a system grown fat, which must become more competitive. Still a third set of observers come with particular nostrums of industrial development banks, and of reconstructions of Depression-form mechanisms to save the old, to foster the new, and to restore the American economic machine.

The very competence of the political system to make hard choices has been questioned. Inflation, and our seemingly limited ability (until recently) to deal with the dollar (at this writing a third of its 1967 value), have been viewed by some observers as true crises of the capacity of a democratic state to absorb current pain in order to secure future stability.

This book is dedicated to an examination of the basic data, to providing a broad range of quantification with which to enable the reader to secure a more neutral perception of the realities. What really has occurred to Americans' income? Are the disaster naysayers justified in terms of the outcomes (incomes and jobs) arising from the melange of economic inputs which have shaped current reality? Are there unique and perhaps transient factors which account for the malaise? Are there better definitions of economic reality than those in common use?

Thus our primary targets in the substantive chapters which follow address the range of approaches involved in measuring the realities of Americans' pockets and of their jobs. This is in no way a comprehensive analysis of trends in productivity, of capital investment, or other data series purported to quantify the underpinning of economic performance, but rather a study of their outcomes. It is the latter which will determine whether the procedures of the past are no longer adequate to deliver an appropriate standard of living, or whether the alarms that have been raised have been overstated. Whether a call for a new economic policy, or virtual revolution in our political institutions, the principal justification has been the assumed failure of the system. With more than a little diffidence, we hope to present an intelligent person's appraisal guide.

CRITICAL EVENTS AND BENCHMARKS

Before doing so, however, it is important to provide a brief historic perspective of critical benchmarks and events that have impacted our recent past and shaped the present. And here once again the limitations of perspective are evident. What is noise and what is the message? The former refers to unique occurrences which, whether for good or ill, are not replicated but rather are absorbed, if painfully; the latter to secular trends which truly channel the future in a relatively immutable fashion. In our opinion there are significant one-of-a-kind shocks in the last dozen years which must be recognized in their impact on the present. But their import may well decline in the future, or have already been buffered. In the latter case, the residual scar tissue may be much more significant historically than as a base for forecasting the future.

The Floating of the Dollar

The 1973 floating of the dollar was a sad tribute to the erosion of its dominant role in the world. America's economic performance and political discipline were no longer adequate to support a fixed value to its currency. From a broad analytical viewpoint, the act may be seen as symbolizing the end of World War II reconstruction, of the rise to full partnership and competitiveness of the traditional European economic base. From yet another perspective, not necessarily in conflict with the first, the rapid growth of the forces that brought the Bretton Woods agreement to an end may have resulted from the failure of the democratic process to accept fiscal reality.[2] Here we have reference to the guns versus butter dispute of the early Viet Nam years; of a President insecure in terms of his political backing, refusing to parallel the war effort with the supporting mechanism of tax policy, thus bringing to an end the era of restrained inflation and dollar stability upon which fixed rates of exchange depended.

From the viewpoint, however, of economic analysis, particularly of efforts to place the American income experience in a world context, floating exchange rates provide yet another variable in efforts at comparative research. As will be detailed in Chapter 2, the vision of American incomes sharply declining when viewed in the setting of our western European neighbors is very substantially a construct of the rates of exchange rather than wholly a functional reality.

The Energy Crises of 1973 and 1979

The full impact of the enormous OPEC-imposed consumption tax on energy, which was the implicit result of the petroleum cost surges of 1973 and 1979, and the transfer of these taxes both domestically and overseas, are still being studied by economists and historians as well. Some observers suggest that other industrial nations (implicitly as a function of their industrial policy) weathered the energy storms better than the United States (i.e., they were able to adapt much more effectively to the new imperatives).[3] A rival argument has been made that, despite partial energy self-sufficiency, the very cheapness and availability of energy in the United States encouraged a production and consumption pattern that, at least in the short run, impacted the country perhaps even more severely than its industrial peers. Historically higher energy prices in Europe and Japan may have buffered the results there. Their productive systems already had been predicated on costly energy, and their products were more aligned to the "new" energy era.[4]

Certainly an American rolling stock of perhaps 100 million automobiles, with gas consumption averaging on the order of 12 miles to the gallon, was rendered obsolete in fairly short order. And this is to say nothing of much of our industrial plant, which was geared to producing these and similar artifacts.

But the two energy shocks now are moving into the domain of the historian. While they leave behind higher costs of energy, much has been done to encyst this wound through capital investment, and indeed inflation itself, though it has been a long, costly and painful process.

Did the recession of 1974-1975, then the worst economic downturn in the post-World War II era, and the even more substantial — and longer lasting — rolling recession of 1980 through 1982, herald the increasing instability of America? Or were they both rather the price of immediate adjustment to the oil shocks? If it is the former — then the system is in trouble. If it is the latter, however, we may view the phenomena not as message, but as a transient happening.

The Flight from Currency and the Rise of the Inflationary Era

The erosion of faith in the competence of the American political system caused by Watergate, and perhaps even by failure in Viet Nam, combined with the energy debacles and the floundering of political will and structure, was symbolized by the era of inflation. Not since Civil War days had a similar crisis of confidence in cash occurred. Its corollary was a flight into the age of collectibles in a fashion highly familiar to those who have worked in the Middle East. Gold and real estate became the touchstones of wealth, while deposits in banks and insurance holdings eroded in value. Resources which historically would have been devoted to investment in productive facilities increasingly were moved to relatively unproductive channels. Fostered by then extant tax policy, the rates of return available to industrial investment in real terms shrank; the siren call of fortunes to be made in collectibles proved ever more alluring.

The cure required by the Federal Reserve's "new" monetarist stance in October 1979 involved a painful reestablishment of the value of currency as interest rates soared. The holding of "hard" assets was rendered much more painful. The virtual collapse of gold and commodity prices in relatively short order was more than paralleled in most of the range of trivia which had served as surrogates for productive investment, whether stamps or beer can collections. The price of earlier political impotence, however, was the severe recession of the early 1980s. In the face of unparalleled interest rates, housing starts, for example, plummeted by more than half; but the runaway inflation attached to housing was finally dispatched. At this writing, price increases of housing are roughly consonant with the overall consumer price index.

Do we view this eruption and its required primitive "cure," of a boom and seemingly deepening bust cycle, as now characteristic of our system? Or are they rather episodes which can be relegated to history? Ominously, the residual level of inflation may be far higher than has held true for most of the post-World War II era.

The Rise of the World Economy

Paralleling, and perhaps accentuated by, all of these events was the rise of a world economy. It is one in which the United States, by many standards at least, has begun to appear less and less competitive. Our poor are relatively affluent compared with the desperation of the lesser-developed nations. Thus the homogenization of world labor markets, and financial markets as well, to say nothing of managerial expertise, has raised significant question as to America's future in labor-intensive activities. The sheer levels of production of our trading partners have risen sharply. Initially this was most clear-cut in the case of western Europe. Increasingly, however, it is evidenced in the countries of the Pacific rim. What is it that Americans will do so uniquely well in the future as to justify their standard of living?

Tax Policy and the New Realism

The demolishing of American complacency in turn generated a variety of adjustments some of whose full implications are still to be felt. These are epitomized by tax policy. The incredible vigor of first generation high-tech company development, immediately after the Sputnik shock of the late 1950s (which created the forerunner of Silicon Valley — the Route 128 prototype in Boston), was brought to a crashing halt very largely by the change in capital gains taxation imposed in 1969. The effective impost was nearly doubled from 25 percent to 49 percent. In 1969, for example, there was $171 million of investment in new start-up companies. By 1975 this had been reduced to $10 million.

While there were other factors at work, it is noticeable that the shift in capital gains taxation back to 28 percent in 1978 (but with a longer holding period required than held true in 1969) in turn was paralleled, after a relatively short lag, by investment of $1.3 billion in new start-up companies by 1981.[5] Similarly, it is difficult to envision the vigor of the tax dimensions of supply side economics and its political potency (which has resulted in very substantial declines in effective corporate imposts) if it were not for the phenomenon of erosion in economic complacency which evolved in the years preceding the 1980 election. Whether these elements will yield a return of consistent long-term vigor to the American economic machine and to all Americans, remains to be seen. But it is evident that the tax strategies of the late 1960s through the late 1970s did not give primary importance to optimizing the performance of the nation's production system. Redistribution was granted far higher priority than economic efficiency.

The Demographic Dilemma

One of the critical events of the 1970s was the absorption of the massive baby boom generation into the economic system. A surge of young people entered the labor force in unprecedented numbers during the decade. The United States in the brief period from 1970 to 1980 added more than 24 million persons to its civilian labor force, an increment nearly equivalent to the total labor force of West Germany.[6] While part of this increase was mirrored in a parallel rise in unemployment — by nearly 4 million from the beginning to the end of the decade — this was dwarfed by a net addition of some 20 million jobs.

Thus the American employment base, i.e., the number of jobs, had to run very rapidly in order to stay in place. This was unlike the situation in western Europe as a whole, where the basic demographics provided much less of a challenge in terms of labor force growth. In periods of economic vigor, the so-called guest workers were absorbed from less affluent parts of Europe and North Africa, only to be largely shifted back in times of downturn. As early as 1961, on the order of 1 percent of the European labor force had taken work in another European country. Typically this was a flow from the South to the industrial areas of western and central Europe, with Switzerland, France and Germany as the dominant host countries. At peak nearly one in ten of the workers in these countries was a migrant — and often with something less than permanent immigration status. A somewhat similar flow has taken place in the United States, with our equivalent the flow across the southern borders or from the Caribbean. But in America they have tended to become permanent residents, adding to the unique native-born bulge in the labor force.[7]

Augmenting the pressure was one of the most significant phenomena of the 1970s: the rise of women in the American labor force. The combination was a unique challenge in time, and one which was largely surmounted. The prime question left behind, however, is whether the downdraft that hit levels of productivity, and the pattern of wage and income distribution, may be a transient phenomenon, a by-product of "indigestion" caused by torrential increases in the size of the labor force and its relative inexperience; or is it rather a chronic issue which will bedevil times to come?

The Rise of a Post-Industrial Society

Agriculture as a dominant form of enterprise and livelihood lasted roughly some 8,000 years. But by the turn of the century in the United States it had been replaced by manufacturing as the single dominant industrial sector. The latter's hegemony came to an end within a single lifetime. By 1950, for example, employment in the service-producing sector (26.7 million) exceeded that of the classic blue collar (goods-producing) sector (18.5 million).[8] And in years following, the evolution of the nation's economic structure was characterized by the industrial/post-industrial shift.

Within our own time, the issue of "deindustrialization," of absolute losses in manufacturing activity within the United States, has been raised.[9] How much of these negative appraisals are a function of generalizations based on downturns within the business cycle as against the evolution of a service economy? To what degree are they supported by longer-term data? (In Chapter 6 these issues are elaborated and appropriate data brought to bear upon them.)

But as the tidal wave of Japanese consumer electronics, of Korean ships, of Brazilian steel, of Indian nails, and of Taiwanese television sets approached our shores, to name but a few of the challenges, the issue of the United States competitiveness has assumed increasing prominence. Whether we were mainly assaulted by cyclical downturns — recession era benchmarks — or were principally impacted by harsh adaptations to new industrial realities — the consequences were mirrored in the nation's income accounts and job profile during the decade.

EXPLANATIONS OF THE PAST: NOSTRUMS FOR THE FUTURE

The series of economic, political and demographic shocks clouding America in the 1970s have spawned a number of diagnoses which have attempted to shed light on why the nation did not fare better than it did. Much, but not all, of the explanation of American economic performance is reduced to theses accounting for productivity (output per hour) gains, or the relative lack thereof, over the past decade.[10] Thus the sections which follow are initiated by a discussion of this variable followed by a sampling of the more prominent expositions of productivity lag.

Productivity

Changes in the levels of American productivity both over time and on a comparative base have been viewed by observers not only as the keys to economic well being, but also as the end results of a variety of inputs. While some of the principal causal mechanisms are briefly outlined below, the reported data are all too clear. The commonly cited statistic is that between 1948 to 1965, annual productivity in the United States increased by 3.2 percent annually; between 1965 and 1973 by 2.4 percent and between 1973 and 1978 by 1.8 percent.[11] Telling comparisons have been made with our international competitors.

International "Catching Up"

The real, as well as statistical, domination of American industry in the immediate post-World War II era represented an unrealistic, artificial baseline from which to view the long-term future. Europe was in shambles, the Far East largely uninvented. Inevitably, as post-war reconstruction ensued — initially heavily underwritten by the United States — American sovereignty diminished. But for almost as long as a generation, competition for our manufactures was minimal. The 1950s and 1960s represented the "golden age" of American prosperity, of undefied productivity advantages.

Knowledge, technology, and expertise, however, are extremely mobile. As the balance of the world industrial order began to build up critical mass, it brought with it challenges to American dominance, altering the historic statistical patterns slowly but substantially. Various *catch-up* theses promulgate this line of reasoning in one form or another. But the foundation of such theses is ultimately one of balance, of stability in relative competitive positions. Will this occur? When does the process end and equilibrium ensue?

Further elaborations attempt to explain unique aspects of national industrial behavior. For example, as late as 1970, the United States accounted for almost 47 percent of the total Gross Domestic Product of the OECD nations, more than five times that of its nearest competitor (Japan).[12] And this was a unique tribute to domestic affluence. The sheer size and scale (and seemingly immutable growth) of the American market made it unnecessary for most U.S. producers to export. As a result, many sectors lulled themselves into poor international competitive postures. The success stories, such as those in the automobile industry, involved relatively autonomous production and styling operations located in host countries.

Foreign manufacturers, strengthened by their own resurgent domestic economies, searched the vast American target for overlooked (or deliberately ignored) niches. And as the mass middle market of United States began to segment during the 1970s, they found themselves particularly well positioned.

The United States had long viewed itself with considerable truth as having a relatively minor involvement in the world economy. By the end of the 1970s, however, this had changed markedly. More than half of our grain, and perhaps 20 percent of our manufacturing employment, was dedicated to overseas markets. Thus, as Reich and Magaziner have suggested, as we enter more forcefully into a world economy, a lack of productivity growth means that American produced goods become less competitive as exports, and similarly, with more and more exposure to foreign competition, the downward pressures on American production for domestic consumption become all too clear.[13]

An ominous feeling of a United States losing its edge is rife in the popular literature. It is important, however, to realize that the difficulties of truly measuring productivity are legendary. Its very breadth permits substantial error and faulty generalization. At best it is increasingly elusive as we move away from the relatively easily counted products of manufacturing to more vague post-industrial outputs. And this is to say nothing of the vagaries of the labor force. Even given all the hard data which can be produced on the elements that ultimately yield to productivity, we are still left with a very limited explanatory capacity; but it is essential that we at least narrow the boundaries of uncertainty.

Productivity and Capital Investment

Technical explanations for the productivity dilemma are certainly not in scarce supply, ranging from the low savings rate in the United States (which supposedly inhibits capital investment) to the substitution of labor for capital in the 1970s due to the sheer scale of the growth in the labor force (resulting from the coming of age of the baby boom). Yet as Thurow points out, "American investment in plant and equipment has risen from 9.5 percent of the GNP during the period between 1948 and 1965 to 11.7 percent of the GNP in the period between 1977 and 1982. The fraction of our resources devoted to gross investment in plant and equipment is up substantially."[14]

At the same time, however, "the amount of capital invested per worker (the capital-labor ratio) is certainly growing more slowly than it used to grow."[15] Thus the baby boom phenomenon surfaces as a potential force underlying the faltering of the economy. Alternatively, the actual distribution of capital spending may have been carried out in less than optimum fashion. This thesis has not only been promulgated by academics such as Reich, but also by the business community invoking the spectre of short-term investment horizons.

Productivity and Management

Some of the political and economic theorizing that has arisen on the productivity issue provides insight to the breadth of its use as a club, for a variety of purposes, with a variety of antecedents. Thus to Bluestone and Harrison, writing under the aegis and funding of major industrial unions, the call for greater levels of productivity, for ironing ''the fat'' out of the system, is nothing but union busting.[16]

Denunciations of the so-called Harvard Business School approach of using discounted cash flow analysis and short-term yield rather than long-term development of competitive vigor and investment are often cited.[17] The best-seller racks are filled with books on the Japanese management miracle and, by definition if not direct intent, of invidious comparisons with American personnel practices, leadership, managerial divorce from the work bench and a whole host of other real and/or supposed sins.

Implicit in all of this however, is the vision that we truly have lost our edge; that this is not merely a phenomenon of unique characteristics of the last decade and a half. There are those who glory in this belief. Thus to some of the neo-Marxists, the United States is involved in a crisis of legitimacy which ultimately will yield the long sought for revolution.[18] A senior *Business Week* editor, while hopeful of ultimate rectification, has somewhat similar indictments of American management. In reviewing the response to OPEC, he suggests that the ''decline of heavy industry in America was aided and abetted by a homegrowth virus: the failure of the U.S. corporate management. When the soaring price of energy began to make the industrial base of much of corporate America obsolete, our managers proved to be totally incompetent . . . the decline of America's industrial heartland was hastened by the incompetence of its corporate managerial elite.''[19]

Governmental Incoherence: The Business Viewpoint

Whether the business community in the broad would fully endorse the latter sentiments is certainly open to question. But their indictment of Washington is clear: government, both implicitly and explicitly, molded an economic environment in the late 1960s and 1970s which retarded business enterprise. Social spending grew at the expense of investment. As noted earlier, tax policy — from the decision to finance the Viet Nam war via inflation to new onerous capital gains tax legislation — set the stage for a decade of vacillation and incoherence in federal economic policy.

Just as Japan and the balance of the industrialized (and developing) world began their economic assault on the United States, our industrial base confronted, successively, wage and price controls, Watergate immobilization, an incoherent and perhaps counterproductive governmental response to the energy crises, embargoes of agricultural exports (soybeans in 1973 and wheat in 1978) which had the functional effect of ceding export markets, futile anti-inflation policies, excessive environmental controls, and a whole host of other misdeeds, both perceived and real. Echoed in the presidential campaign of 1980, the call for the future was the provision of a stable and predictable economic environment — and "freeing American enterprise from the burdens of irrational government control." A primary debate of the present and future is exemplified by the tensions in the Democratic party between income redistributional foci and the requirements for economic growth.

The Industrial Policy Dilemma

During the depths of the 1982 recession, the industrial policy debate — the need for conscious industrial strategies — reached full force, becoming a staple of the popular media.[20] Some observers suggest that we already have an industrial policy, represented in part by the governmental activities tabulated above — inadvertent byproducts of all manner of public actions.[21] The failure to implement an explicit and coherent industrial policy — special treatment for high technology sectors of the American economy and aided restructuring of distressed industries in a strategic planning framework — is seen as the primary cause of the nation's shifting international competitive position.

Hardening of the Arteries

Is it just middle-age? Much of these arguments is amplified by indictments of the political/social system. Thus Mancur Olsen in the *Rise and Decline of Nations* suggests that the older a political organization becomes, the more encrusted it becomes with special interest groups. Unless these are broad enough to encompass the nation, they tend to be irresponsible, each of them seeking out its own preferential status, despite the cost of aggregate overall vigor. He suggests in this context that the relative success of Germany and Japan resulted from the crushing of extant special interest groups through their national reorganization after World War II. The somber tenor of his remarks is indicated by the following summary: "Neither of the political parties can make the economy work any longer because the special interests are more numerous than ever; neither the left wing nor the right wing ideologies recognize this."[22]

It is striking to note that at a somewhat different end of the political spectrum, Robert Lekachman, one of the leading liberal left economists of our time, has suggested a very strong parallel rising between United States and England — essentially a phenomenon of tired blood, of expertise perhaps in avant-garde research but with a lack of implementing capacity. He suggests that the United States is replaying the British parallel when "in the 1880's, for no adequate reason, these aggressive thrusting souls lost their elan, became complacent, and gradually lost ground to American and German rivals.''[23] And indeed Robert Reich, one of the strongest critics of American capital investment procedures, has similarly raised the same issue questioning the capacity of our major political parties, both Republican and Democratic, to avoid drowning industrial policy in the pork barrel.[24]

FUTURE PERSPECTIVES: NEW PARAMETERS?

Certainly the mapping of what really is taking place, and what has taken place, in the economic sphere's sticky terrain is much more than merely intellectual sport. Varying visions of the past and present provide alternate bases and matrices for future policy. This is increasingly important as the pressure of advancing high technology begins to dominate the scene: robotics and computer-aided manufacturing on the factory floor and equally striking and important contrivances reducing the requirements for human input in the office.

Many of the generalizations of what was happening in the American economy (and by definition would continue to happen) were radically altered with the policy reversals of the post-1979 years. Thus much of the criticism of America's economy is based on factors which may have shifted markedly in recent years. It is essential that the key elements of the new matrix be kept in mind as we attempt to grasp the future.

The Resurgence of the Dollar

The wild peregrinations of the dollar within the international currency landscape — to say nothing of its relationship to gold itself — provides one of the most dramatic reversals in monetary history. The path from its overheated days at the close of the 1960s (which as we have suggested, marked the termination of the immediate post-World War II era) to its nadir at the end of the decade of the 1970s, only to be followed by an unparalleled resurgence in the early 1980s, has confounded analysts, traders, and policymakers alike. The dollar continuing as the world currency of choice, in the face of enormous deficits both in the federal budget as well as in international trade, is a tale viewed much more with awe than true comprehension. The relative value of the currency is both a reflection of underlying economic reality and a key independent variable. Without question, therefore, both for good or ill, it provides one of the more powerful shapers of the future. The changes in the dollar's value in this decade so far provide a mirror image of those of the 1970s; but how long will this continue?

The Enfeeblement of OPEC

Again, the abrupt discontinuities between the recent past and current events are highlighted by the changing status of OPEC and its underpinnings, the price and availability of energy. To some observers what has occurred is highly reminiscent of the Greek concept of hubris, the sin of overweening pride:

> By raising the price of energy so sharply and so quickly, OPEC transformed the entire base of the world economy. . . . changed the technological foundations of Western society and set in motion vast social and political changes that are only now coming into focus . . . [and] speeded up the entire process of transformation to a blinding rate. . . . All this was an accident, an unintended event. History is full of ironies, of course, and surely this must be one of its choicest. By raising oil prices so quickly and so sharply, OPEC set off the technological and economic changes that buried it — with equal dispatch.[25]

The crisis atmosphere of energy shortfalls and cost surges which punctuated the last decade, marked by the gas lines of 1974 and the soaring prices of 1979, has given way to energy complacency. Consumption has stabilized and the seemingly immutable relationship between GNP growth and increasing usage of energy has, for the moment, abated. Many of the costly emergency energy-independence programs — the shale oil projects, heavy oil developments, to say nothing of the entire range of synfuel programs — have not merely been mothballed, but rather relegated to costly memory. But this too must be viewed with some question, given the political instability which characterizes so much of the oil-rich regions of the world.

The price of reducing OPEC's hegemony was a worldwide economic slowdown. Have the lessons of the past been learned thoroughly enough? Or will future historians find that as the United States and its trading partners fully emerged from the depths of the 1982 recession, a return to profligacy ensued? And at what price? Will the latter part of the 1980s show that we have been able to surmount the OPEC challenge?

The Inflationary Question

The initial stabilization and subsequent decline in the price of energy have been crucial to the muting of the inflationary cycle within the United States. At the cost of a very sharp and painful recession, annual increments in the consumer price index were brought down in the early 1980s to a third of their peak levels of the 1970s. It must be noted, however, that this has still yielded a relatively high inflation plateau — indeed one which is comparable to that of a decade earlier (at the beginning of the 1970s), which invoked President Nixon's imposing price and wage controls. The battle is far from over, its future prospects more than a little unclear at this writing. The impact of current inflation, however, comes upon a scene which has been much altered by the dismal experience of the past decade.

The New Tax and Investment Matrix

The United States (whether for good or ill) has adapted its financial and tax mechanisms to coping with — if not surmounting — an inflationary constant. While some of these changes have been touched on before, it should be noted that the inflation of the last decade was accentuated in its deleterious effects by the lack of buffer mechanisms in the fiscal arena. Thus for much of the 1970s, real rates of return on debt, to say nothing of investment, were negative. Corporate profitability was drastically overstated because of inadequate depreciation allowances. Much of the nominal taxable profits of business actually represented a decline in the capital base of the country as replacement costs were drastically understated. High marginal rates of taxation created turbulence in the floating of indebtedness forcing high coupon costs to counter the tax and inflation biases.

While certainly the structure currently in place could not withstand runaway inflation, it is equally evident that it is much more competent to cope with low levels of erosion than heretofore have been the case. The very indexation, however, which now pervades the American economy, the homogenization of financial markets, interest rates and the like, raises some issues of the adequacy of damping forces as we face the future.

Changing Demographics

The demographic-workforce profile of the United States will shift very rapidly in the future. The civilian labor force bulge of the 1970s yielded an unparalleled increment of 2.4 million participants annually. The decade terminating in 1990, however, will impose much less of a strain on the absorptive capacity of our economic mechanisms — with an average annual labor force growth of only 1.8 million, a decline of a full 25 percent. And if we look even further ahead to the 1990 to 1995 era, most projections envision the labor force growing by only 1.2 million persons per year.[26] If historic trends hold, this should be a uniquely productive era for America's labor force with the drastic reduction in newcomers accompanied by a baby boom generation maturing into its prime working years.

The Lean-Mean Economic Machine

Recessions have always served as a purge — if a painful one — of business in America. While typically there is some lag in the reduction of costs to meet lowered volume, a standardized pattern traditionally is followed. Companies initially discover that there are many functions — and functionaries — that they can do without. The years of plenty had tended to be accompanied by add-ons in both personnel and process which are redundant; breakeven points had ratcheted upward, paralleling staffing growth (and perhaps some level of luxury in the corporate suite). A whole range of elements become eligible for pruning.

The experience of harsh times, which for many manufacturing firms now nearly is a decade old, has imposed a very vigorous discipline on American corporate society. Breakeven points, both in terms of units as well as dollar volume, have been substantially reduced for much of our heavy industry. A *Wall Street Journal* study indicates that domestic automobile manufacturers as a group, as of 1983, could break even on a third fewer units than held true in the late 1970s.[27] Productivity increases are suddenly soaring in selected smokestack industries.[28] The return of essentials is highlighted by the new respect and status given competence in manufacturing in the executive suite. In the era of regulation, the latter was increasingly dominated by lawyers, or by management with financial backgrounds. For the first time in a generation, individuals with production backgrounds are increasingly significant as prospects for top corporate positions.[29]

The New Heroes

The vision of American corporate society of a decade ago was one of relative production stagnancy, an emphasis on consumption. The new fortunes in America tended to be concentrated in fast foods and other areas of consumer services. The heroes of today increasingly are the entrepreneurs of technology. The Ray Krocs of McDonald's still have many parallels — but primacy in the media are given the Steven Jobs of Apple Computers, the leaders of Tandon and of Intel, firms which represent the cutting edge of America's international economic competence.

Fortified by the changes in capital gains taxation earlier described, America's new venture activity is now the envy of the rest of the world. While many in the United States look to MITI as an instrument to bring economic priorities and order from on-high into the American scene, the Japanese, the Germans, and the French as well as the British all view, with a combination both of awe and in some cases dread, the sheer vitality of the new high-tech companies whose leaders have rapidly become the new folk heroes of America.[30] Even in college bookstores such works as *In Search of Excellence* have achieved best-sellerdom. Business schools are bulging, if unfortunately at the cost of less immediately rewarding topics.[31]

One would have to go back to the years immediately following Sputnik to see a parallel. The revival of corporate America's respectability after the Watergate era is evident. Its longevity, however, depends upon its delivering the goods. Will it be able to cope effectively with the future? Can it maintain a constructive long-term relationship with organized labor, increasingly insecure in the face of uncertainty?

The imperatives of budget deficits, of trade gap closure, and of the world financial crisis itself, with its sad spectre of protectionism, all provide challenges to a positive future. In a mood of "back to basics," reappraisal of our key economic building blocks is called for. The chapters which follow are a modest effort in this direction, focusing on the realities of incomes and jobs in the United States, the limitations of our measuring tools, and the dangers of selective choice among them.

NOTES

1. A general measurement used for international comparative income analysis is gross domestic product per capita. This statistic, however, is subject to substantial variation when converted to a common measuring system. Currency exchange rate assumptions, and inflation-standardizing assumptions, have significant impact in this regard. The percentages cited in the text were based on data converted to dollars via the exchange rates and price levels of 1975. Chapter 2 presents a full elaboration of the alternatives and the wide range of variations that result.

2. "Bretton Woods" has become a common reference to the landmark meeting of wartime leaders in Bretton Woods, New Hampshire in 1944, that created fixed exchange rates among major currencies. A major foundation of the system was an American guarantee to convert dollars into gold at $35 an ounce. In 1971, the agreement lapsed when the U.S. terminated dollar-to-gold conversions. Fixed exchange rates were terminated in 1973.

3. See: Robert B. Reich, "An Industrial Policy of the Right," *The Public Interest*, No. 73, Fall 1983, p. 11.

4. Also, OPEC price hikes may have been mitigated in Europe (and Japan) by the declining value of the U.S. dollar in the 1970s; since oil is denominated in U.S. dollars, they were shielded from the full vigor of the price hikes.

5. The capital gains and investment figures were secured from Bruce Nussbaum, *The World After Oil* (New York: Simon and Schuster, 1983) p. 284.

6. The civilian labor force in West Germany in 1980 comprised 26 million people, virtually identical to the total in 1970 (26.1 million people). See: Organization for Economic Cooperation and Development, *Labor Force Statistics: 1969-1980*, Paris, 1982.

In the United States, the civilian labor force increased from 82.8 million persons in 1970 to 106.9 million in 1980. This growth, while mainly the result of the maturing baby boom bulge entering into its working age years, was also bolstered by the increasing labor force participation rate of women during the decade. See: Bureau of Labor Statistics, *Monthly Labor Review* (monthly).

7. A smaller and later baby boom influx into the labor force has been suggested as a cause of Europe's economic difficulties in the early 1980s. For example, there has been a growth in the German labor force — after a decade of stability — as a result of large numbers of young people entering the labor force; the latter are confronted with a decreasing number of jobs. See: Werner Heintz, "Urban Policy in the Federal Republic of Germany," in Gail Garfield Schwartz, ed., *Advanced Industrialization in the Inner Cities* (Lexington, MA: Lexington Books, 1981) p. 126.

8. "Goods-producing" includes mining, construction and manufacturing. "Service-producing" includes transportation and public utilities; wholesale and retail trade; finance, insurance, and real estate; services; and government.

9. By 1980, manufacturing employment (20.285 million) fell below that of wholesale and retail trade alone (20.310 million). Thus the United States now has more people engaged in trading and selling goods than in producing them.

10. Productivity is defined by the Bureau of Labor Statistics as the constant dollar gross domestic product produced in a given period divided by the number of hours worked. It measures the value of goods and services produced per hour of labor.

11. Robert B. Reich, *op. cit.*, p. 9.

12. The percentage is somewhat suspect, as indicated in Chapter 2. OECD stands for Organization for Economic Cooperation and Development, comprising the major industrialized countries. Chapter 2 fully details its composition.

13. Ira C. Magaziner and Robert D. Reich, *Minding America's Business: The Decline and Rise of the American Economy* (New York: Harcourt Brace Jovanovich, 1982) p. 36.

14. Lester C. Thurow. "The Elephant and the Maharajah." *The New York Review of Books*, Volume XXX, Number 20, December 22, 1983, p. 48.

15. *Ibid*. Thurow explains the dilemma as follows: "The average American worker uses about $58,000 worth of plant and equipment (in 1982 dollars). To have the average American productivity a worker must have that $58,000 in equipment. But this means that if America had a baby boom twenty years ago, parents were implicitly promising not just to bathe, feed, and educate their babies but that approximately twenty years later they would stop and save $58,000. This would provide the capital to equip each of their babies (and their wives) to enter the labor force as average American workers. And it is precisely this implicit promise we Americans aren't keeping."

16. Barry Bluestone and Bennett Harrison, *The Deindustrialization of America* (New York: Basic Books, 1982).

17. Magaziner and Reich, *op. cit.*, Chapter 8.

18. See, for example, Bennett Harrison's response to a critic from the left on *The Deindustrialization of America* in *Antipode*, Volume 14, Number 2, 1982, pp. 47-52.

19. Nussbaum, *op. cit.* p. 259, 261. A variation of this perspective is provided in: Paul Hawken, *The Next Economy* (New York: Holt, Rinehart and Winston, 1983). The major scholarly criticism was presented in William J. Abernathy and Robert Hayes, "Managing Our Way to Economic Decline," *Harvard Business Review*, July-August 1980.

20. The term industrial policy, unfortunately, means different things to different people. The following is a brief synopsis of several of the more common parameters of the term:

a. A governmental focus on the most productive patterns of investment — accelerating changes in promising (sunrise) industries already signaled by the marketplace — assisting the transition from R & D to efficient production process.
b. Government targeting of specific industrial sectors as potential new growth engines — the provision of research support at early conceptual stages.
c. Public adjustment policies focusing on declining (sunset) industries designed to minimize pain and dislocation via retraining and other support programs.
d. Government central planning and the formulation of growth-oriented macro policies.

21. An overview of industrial policy alternatives is presented in Magaziner and Reich, *op. cit.* For related discussions, see: George Gilder, "A Supply-Side Economics of the Left," *The Public Interest*, Number 72, Summer 1983, pp. 26-43, and Amitai Etzioni, "The MITIzation of America?", *The Public Interest*, Number 72, Summer 1983, pp. 44-51.

22. Mancur Olson, *The Rise and Decline of Nations: Economic Growth, Stagflation and Social Rigidities* (New Haven: Yale University Press, 1982). For a very good precis, see: *Resources* (Resources for the Future) No. 72, February 1983, pp. 2-3.

23. Robert Lekachman, *Greed is Not Enough: Reaganomics* (New York: Pantheon Books, 1982) p. 69.

24. Reich, *op. cit.*, p. 9.

25. Nussbaum, *op. cit.*, p. 63.

26. For labor force projections, see: Howard N. Fullerton, Jr. and John Tschetter, "The 1995 Labor Force: A Second Look," *Monthly Labor Review*, Volume 106, Number 11, November 1983, pp. 3-10. See also Chapter 6.

27. Robert L. Simison and John Koten, "High Gear Profits: Auto Makers' Earnings Are Increasing Sharply Despite Mediocre Sales." *The Wall Street Journal*, Monday, December 19, 1983, pp. 1, 19.

28. *Ibid*. Ford's North American production in 1983 rose to about 27 vehicles per worker compared to 18 in 1979.

29. John Holusha, "The New Allure of Manufacturing." *The New York Times*, Section 3 (Business), Sunday, December 18, 1983, pp. 1, 30.

30. MITI (Ministry of International Trade and Industry) is a Japanese advisory council that serves as a mechanism for consensus-forming among the major Japanese economic constituencies. For the growing recognition in the media of the entrepreneur, see: "Macro Maestros," *Time*, Volume 121,

Number 1, January 3, 1983, pp. 25-29, and "The New Entrepreneurs," *Business Week*, April 18, 1983, pp. 78-88.

31. Thomas J. Peters and Robert H. Waterman, Jr., *In Search of Excellence* (New York: Harper and Row, 1982).

Chapter Two

INTERNATIONAL INCOME COMPARISONS

The United States is undergoing a period of self-examination of its economy and attendant institutions unparalleled since the era of the Great Depression. A crucial debate is being waged as to whether conventional economic instruments, and government relationships with the private business sector, are adequate to meet the growing challenge of rival nations. The crisis of confidence which has developed is exemplified by assertions that the United States is rapidly falling behind other countries in terms of productivity and income levels. In the course of this debate, a variety of data on national income has been used for illustrative purposes. Unfortunately, single dimensions of complex statistical reality can tend to mislead as well as provide insight.

In the presentation which follows, some of the vagaries of assessing income are highlighted. The material is far from exhaustive; it does however, provide an introduction to a most important set of measuring tools. The issues of America's economic future are much too important to tolerate misleading generalizations. It is essential that our national self-analysis be conducted within a framework of appropriate measuring tools. Within this context the analyses which follow may serve as a useful introduction.

MEASURING AND COMPARING GROSS DOMESTIC PRODUCT PER CAPITA

In an international framework, gross domestic product (GDP) is one of the best standardized gauges of national income. It measures the value of the flow of goods and services produced *within* a country, differing from gross national product (GNP) in its exclusion of income or remittances generated by investments from abroad (gross product originating outside a nation). Thus it provides a measurement of a society's domestic income generation. (National income, which by its very label would appear to be a more appropriate indicator, subtracts capital consumption allowances, i.e., depreciation, and indirect business taxes. Since these factors exhibit wide international variations, GDP has become a standard convention for international comparisons.) Gross domestic product per capita provides a further standardization by making possible an income per person parameter.

Making international comparisons of GDP per capita still is far from a routine exercise. Conversions to a common currency standard and corrections for inflation are handled in different ways and produce disparate conclusions. In the first six tabular presentations of this chapter, the analyses of three different approaches to these concerns are undertaken.

EXHIBIT 1
Gross Domestic Product Per Capita, in U.S. Dollars — at Current Prices and 1975 Exchange Rates: U.S. and Selected Nations, 1969 to 1981

	1969	1971	1973	1975	1977	1979	1981
United States	4,641	5,168	6,207	7,125	8,641	10,585	12,647
Belgium	3,208	3,885	4,898	6,300	7,696	8,795	9,743
Canada	3,764	4,342	5,547	7,214	8,948	11,087	13,841
Denmark	3,817	4,598	5,990	7,438	9,553	11,798	14,070
France	3,249	3,971	4,987	6,429	8,284	10,643	13,378
Germany	4,039	4,978	6,016	6,748	7,918	9,224	10,174
Japan	2,048	2,571	3,485	4,473	5,459	6,357	7,138
Netherlands	3,285	4,086	5,202	6,377	7,846	8,900	9,730
Sweden	4,611	5,514	6,687	8,814	10,720	13,304	16,469
Switzerland	5,076	6,309	7,835	8,477	8,927	9,676	11,245
United Kingdom	1,855	2,270	2,877	4,129	5,673	7,629	9,782

Source: Organization for Economic Cooperation and Development (OECD), Department of Economics and Statistics, *National Accounts: 1952-1981*, Paris, 1982.

GDP at Current Prices and 1975 Exchange Rates

As published by the Organization for Economic Cooperation and Development (OECD), Exhibit 1 presents GDP per capita for the United States and ten nations at two-year intervals between 1969 and 1981.[1] The data are not corrected for inflation; thus current prices are directly converted to U.S. dollars by the

EXHIBIT 2
Gross Domestic Product Per Capita as a Percent of U.S. Gross Domestic Product per Capita — at Current Prices and 1975 Exchange Rates

	1969	1971	1973	1975	1977	1979	1981
Belgium	69	75	79	88	89	83	77
Canada	81	84	89	101	104	105	109
Denmark	82	89	97	104	111	111	111
France	70	77	80	90	96	101	106
Germany	87	96	97	95	92	87	80
Japan	44	50	56	63	63	60	56
Netherlands	71	79	84	90	91	84	77
Sweden	99	107	108	124	124	126	130
Switzerland	109	122	126	119	103	91	89
United Kingdom	40	44	46	58	66	72	77

Source: Organization for Economic Cooperation and Development (OECD), Department of Economics and Statistics, *National Accounts: 1952-1981*, Paris, 1982.

1975 exchange rates for the respective nations' currencies. According to the resulting dollar per capita GDPs, in 1981 the United States ($12,647), ranked well behind Sweden ($16,469), Denmark ($14,070), Canada ($13,841), and France ($13,378). In 1969, the United States ($4,641) had lagged only Switzerland ($5,076), indicating a significant relative decline in the economic position of the U.S. and its citizenry.

To facilitate trendline analysis, Exhibit 2 presents a set of indices which represent each nation's gross national product per capita as a percent of U.S. GDP per capita. Sweden's GDP per capita in 1969, for example, was 99 percent that of the U.S.; by 1981, it was 130 percent. It is interesting to note that Japan had shown no overall progress from 1973 — the year of the first oil embargo — to 1981, despite brief interim gains. Again, by this latter year, the Japanese GDP per capita was less than three-fifths (56 percent) that of the United States. Even Germany was at only the four-fifths level (80 percent) and, indeed, had degenerated since 1969 on a comparative base (87 percent). Over the same period, the United Kingdom, often jocularly referred to as the first NSN (Newly Submerging Nation), saw its GDP per capita rise from 40 percent that of the U.S. in 1969 to 77 percent by 1981.

The decline in the stature of Germany and the rise in position of the United Kingdom appear distinctly at odds with the general perception of the past decade. This and other apparent ''anomalies'' are mainly due to the utilization of current prices in the data set and the use of fixed 1975 exchange rates. High rates of inflation will inflate the nominal GDP levels, and thus exaggerate economic per-

EXHIBIT 3
Gross Domestic Product Per Capita, in Constant U.S. Dollars — at the Exchange Rates and Price Levels of 1975: U.S. and Selected Nations, 1969 to 1981

	1969	1971	1973	1975	1977	1979	1981
United States	6,734	6,754	7,361	7,125	7,712	8,087	8,078
Belgium	5,076	5,573	6,187	6,300	6,694	7,051	7,123
Canada	5,961	6,372	7,095	7,214	7,630	8,037	8,208
Denmark	6,822	7,047	7,625	7,438	8,063	8,459	8,365
France	5,236	5,729	6,286	6,429	6,919	7,363	7,392
Germany	5,925	6,313	6,795	6,748	7,383	7,930	8,056
Japan	3,539	3,936	4,530	4,473	4,855	5,268	5,589
Netherlands	5,426	5,893	6,324	6,377	6,777	7,015	6,895
Sweden	7,463	7,880	8,323	8,814	8,679	9,124	9,203
Switzerland	7,892	8,583	8,976	8,477	8,667	8,890	9,413
United Kingdom	3,682	3,841	4,200	4,129	4,336	4,566	4,382

Source: Organization for Economic Cooperation and Development (OECD), Department of Economics and Statistics, *National Accounts: 1952-1981*, Paris, 1982.

EXHIBIT 4
Gross Domestic Product Per Capita as a Percent of U.S. Gross Domestic Product Per Capita — at the Exchange Rates and Price Levels of 1975

	1969	1971	1973	1975	1977	1979	1981
Belgium	75	83	84	88	87	87	88
Canada	89	94	96	101	99	99	102
Denmark	101	104	104	104	105	105	104
France	78	85	85	90	90	91	92
Germany	88	93	92	95	96	98	100
Japan	53	58	62	63	63	65	69
Netherlands	81	87	86	90	88	87	85
Sweden	111	117	113	124	113	113	114
Switzerland	117	127	122	119	112	110	117
United Kingdom	55	57	57	58	56	56	54

Source: Organization for Economic Cooperation and Development (OECD), Department of Economics and Statistics, *National Accounts: 1952-1981*, Paris, 1982.

formance vis-à-vis low inflation countries, e.g., France versus Germany in the post-1977 period (see Exhibit 2).[2] And since in this example, exchange rates are fixed at their 1975 level, they do not offer a counterbalancing "correction" to inflationary "bonuses," i.e., currencies in high inflation nations will, other things being equal, decline in value against those of more stable countries.

GDP at the Exchange Rates and Price Levels of 1975

In Exhibits 3 and 4, the same basic data formats are replicated but are now standardized for inflation by using both the exchange rates and price levels of 1975. (The data in Exhibit 3 are as published by OECD.) As would be guessed, the results are substantially different. Switzerland, for example, reflecting its low inflation rate, becomes the top-rated nation in 1981, moving from 89 percent of U.S. GDP per capita (Exhibit 2) to 117 percent (Exhibit 4). Sweden falls back quite sharply from 130 to 114. Even more striking is the comparison in the data for the United Kingdom. The severe inflation which that country experienced is indicated by its decline from 77 percent of the 1981 U.S. equivalent under current price level conversions (Exhibit 2) to little more than half — 54 percent — under constant 1975 price conversions (Exhibit 4). Japan, which before (Exhibit 2) had been at the 56 percent mark, now with a correction for inflation moves up to the 69 percent level (Exhibit 4). And the relative positions of Germany and France have been reversed. Nonetheless, the long-term diminution of the economic standing of the U.S. is again pictured. But that is far from the end of the story. A major question is whether the exchange rates of 1975 adequately reflect the economic reality of the present.

EXHIBIT 5
Gross Domestic Product Per Capita, in U.S. Dollars — at Current Prices and Exchange Rates: U.S. and Selected Nations, 1969 to 1981

	1969	1971	1973	1975	1977	1979	1981
United States	4,641	5,168	6,207	7,125	8,641	10,585	12,647
Belgium	2,353	2,944	4,622	6,300	7,897	11,033	9,651
Canada	3,555	4,373	5,640	7,214	8,557	9,626	11,741
Denmark	2,917	3,567	5,690	7,438	9,144	12,886	11,350
France	2,679	3,088	4,800	6,429	7,226	10,723	10,552
Germany	2,532	3,517	5,538	6,748	8,389	12,381	11,076
Japan	1,696	2,193	3,806	4,473	6,034	8,609	9,606
Netherlands	2,292	2,957	4,706	6,377	8,085	11,220	9,861
Sweden	3,703	4,482	6,357	8,814	9,932	12,885	13,505
Switzerland	3,038	3,958	6,387	8,477	9,587	15,021	14,778
United Kingdom	2,005	2,507	3,187	4,129	4,473	7,304	8,886

Source: Organization for Economic Cooperation and Development (OECD), Department of Economics and Statistics, *National Accounts: 1952-1981*, Paris, 1982.

EXHIBIT 6
Gross Domestic Product Per Capita as a Percent of U.S. Gross Domestic Product Per Capita — at Current Prices and Exchange Rates

	1969	1971	1973	1975	1977	1979	1981
Belgium	51	57	74	88	91	104	76
Canada	77	85	91	101	99	91	93
Denmark	63	69	92	104	106	122	90
France	58	60	77	90	84	101	83
Germany	55	68	89	95	97	117	88
Japan	37	42	61	63	70	81	76
Netherlands	49	57	76	90	94	106	78
Sweden	80	87	102	124	115	122	107
Switzerland	65	77	103	119	111	142	117
United Kingdom	43	49	51	58	52	69	70

Source: Organization for Economic Cooperation and Development (OECD), Department of Economics and Statistics, *National Accounts: 1952-1981*, Paris, 1982.

GDP at Current Prices and Exchange Rates

If we were to implement an analysis for the same countries over the same period of time, but now utilize *current* prices and *current* exchange rates — i.e., *the exchange rates and price levels which were operative for each specific year* — a very different relative positioning would emerge, and perhaps a more realistic one. (As presented by OECD, the use of current exchange rates ostensibly limits the need for direct inflation correction, since changes in exchange rates are to some degree a function of relative rates of inflation.) As detailed in Exhibits 5 and 6, now only Sweden and Switzerland — with GDPs per capita at 107 and 117 percent that of United States — exceed the United States benchmark.

Certainly, however, a substantial degeneration in the decade since 1969 in the U.S. position, as gauged by these criteria, had taken place. By 1979, for example, fully seven out of the 10 countries for which data are presented exceeded the United States in GDP per capita (Exhibit 5). But there was a very signal relative U.S. improvement from 1979 to 1981. Over the two-year period Japan shrank from 81 percent of U.S. GDP per capita down to 76 percent; Sweden from 122 to 107; and France and Germany, perhaps even more significantly, from above the 100 mark to 83 and 88 percent, respectively (Exhibit 6). Generalizations based on the data shown here would suggest that the United States, after a decade of comparative retreat, has suddenly reversed the field.

EXHIBIT 7
Foreign Exchange Rates: 1969 to 1982
(In U.S. cents per unit of foreign currency)

	Currency Unit	1969	1971	1973	1975	1977	1979	1981	1982
Belgium	Franc	1.99	2.06	2.58	2.73	2.79	3.41	2.70	2.18
Canada	Dollar	92.86	99.02	99.98	98.30	94.11	85.39	83.41	81.01
Denmark	Krone	13.30	13.51	16.60	17.44	16.66	19.01	14.08	11.98
France	Franc	19.30	18.15	22.54	23.35	20.34	23.50	18.49	15.20
Germany	Deutsche mark	25.49	28.77	37.76	40.73	43.09	54.56	44.36	41.19
Japan	Yen	0.28	0.29	0.37	0.34	0.37	0.46	0.45	0.40
Netherlands	Guilder	27.59	28.65	35.98	39.63	40.75	49.84	40.19	37.43
Sweden	Krona	19.34	19.59	22.97	24.14	22.38	23.32	19.86	15.91
Switzerland	Franc	23.19	24.33	31.70	38.74	41.71	60.12	51.03	49.20
United Kingdom	Pound	239.01	244.42	245.10	222.16	174.49	212.24	202.43	174.80

Source: Board of Governors of the Federal Reserve System, *Federal Reserve Bulletin*, monthly.

THE EXCHANGE RATE DILEMMA

There are two major elements at work which underlie the variations that have been discussed. The more frequently cited of the two is the impact of turbulent foreign exchange rates. When we measure a country's production or income within its own currency — and then transmute this figure into American dollars — the relative shifts in exchange rates over time may play a far larger role than actual changes in the physical quanta of production or income per se.

Exhibit 7 illustrates the sharp changes which have taken place in foreign exchange rates from 1969 through 1982; the data are defined in terms of U.S. cents-per-unit of foreign currency. The patterns reveal the abrupt transition initially from the baseline of 1969 (whose foundation was set nearly a generation before in the Bretton Woods agreement which essentially fixed the price of currencies) and the revolution which took place during 1971 (the end of the era of fixed exchange rates).[3] In the brief four-year period from 1969 to 1973, for example, the value of the yen increased by nearly a third against the dollar and the deutsche mark by nearly half. Indeed, the dollar sank against every one of the rival currencies shown in Exhibit 7. This process essentially continued through 1979. By that year, the dollar once again had lost substantially to the deutsche mark, with the latter moving from a value of 37.76 cents in 1973 up past the 54-cent mark. The yen, similarly, moved from 37 to 46 cents. With the exception of the British pound and the Canadian dollar, 1979 — at least at this writing — seems to have been the high-water mark of foreign currencies — and conversely, the low-water mark of the dollar. And much of the reporting of America's decline has been based on this period.

The abrupt reversal which has taken place since then is shown in the far right of the exhibit. The franc, for example, is off by nearly a third. The deutsche mark has retreated back close to its 1975 level, and the yen is off by 15 percent from its peak figure. And these trends persisted through all of 1983.

The impact of these vagaries on the nominal reporting of gross domestic product, and with it measures of income and indeed of the very health of the economy as a whole, needs little illustration. Much of the comparative decline of United States' growth in the decade ending in 1979 resulted from the questionable caliber of the measuring sticks which have been applied to it when contrasting its vitality to the other principal industrial powers.

In 1969, the dollar was grossly overvalued — a result of the overdelayed readjustment of the Bretton Woods formula. At that time, and during the preceding two decades, the use of official exchange rates tended to understate the level of real GDP in European countries compared to the United States. Thus the 1969 baseline for gauging present economic postures sets the U.S. position at an artificially high starting point, since "the official exchange rates used to convert European currencies to dollars considerably understate[d] the relative purchasing powers of these currencies and consequently seriously distort[ed] the comparison of the levels of real national product in Europe with that in the United States.''[4]

By 1979, after eight years of floating exchange rates, the dollar was severely undervalued. Certainly the period from 1979 through 1982 would confirm this impression as other currencies sank in contrast to that of the United States (Exhibit 7). Thus, even if there had been no shift in physical production within the several countries under discussion, the simple valuation of this production in local currencies — and the shift in the value of those currencies against the dollar — would generate somewhat spurious conclusions on the relative weakness of the United States, and the relative vigor of the other countries discussed here.

EXHIBIT 8
Total Population, U.S. and Selected Nations: 1969-1980
(Numbers in thousands)

			Change: 1969-80	
	1969	**1980**	**Number**	**Percent**
United States	202,677	227,627	24,950	12.3
Belgium	9,613	9,859	246	2.6
Canada	21,028	23,959	2,931	13.9
Denmark	4,893	5,125	232	4.7
France	50,315	53,713	3,398	6.8
Germany	60,067	61,566	1,499	2.5
Japan	102,320	116,782	14,462	14.1
Netherlands	12,878	14,150	1,272	9.9
Sweden	7,968	8,311	343	4.3
Switzerland	6,212	6,373	161	2.6
United Kingdom	55,372	56,010	638	1.2
OECD Europe	365,830	394,173	28,343	7.7
EEC	258,493	270,857	12,364	4.8
OECD Total	706,898	780,288	73,390	10.4

Source: Organization for Economic Cooperation and Development (OECD), Department of Economics and Statistics, *Labor Force Statistics: 1969-1980*, Paris, 1982.

THE INFLUENCE OF DEMOGRAPHICS

The difficulties of measurement are further complicated, when we deal in per capita terms, by the changing demographic profiles of various countries. In Exhibit 8, for example, is shown the total population of the United States and

EXHIBIT 9
GDP Per Capita in Current U.S. Dollars Using Current PPPs (U.S. Dollars): U.S. and Selected Nations 1970 to 1981

	1970	1971	1973	1975	1977	1979	1980	1981
United States	4,822	5,168	6,207	7,125	8,641	10,585	11,416	12,647
Belgium	3,322	3,624	4,432	5,356	6,382	7,861	8,848	9,495
Canada	N.A.	—	—	—	—	—	—	—
Denmark	3,843	4,122	4,914	5,688	6,914	8,483	9,167	10,031
France	3,441	3,787	4,579	5,558	6,694	8,290	9,150	9,981
Germany	3,674	3,959	4,696	5,534	6,789	8,528	9,475	10,360
Japan	3,060	3,298	4,184	4,898	5,958	7,552	8,556	9,583
Netherlands	3,612	3,924	4,640	5,553	6,617	8,010	8,773	9,414
Sweden	N.A.	—	—	—	—	—	—	—
Switzerland	N.A.	—	—	—	—	—	—	—
United Kingdom	3,282	3,540	4,265	4,976	5,859	7,217	7,730	8,281

Source: Organization for Economic Cooperation and Development (OECD), Department of Economics and Statistics, *National Accounts: 1952-1981*, Paris, 1982.

other selected nations from 1969 through 1980. With the exception of Canada, only Japan exceeded the United States' increase of 12.3 percent in the 11-year period under consideration. The population levels of Germany, of Switzerland, of the United Kingdom and of Belgium were essentially stable, with growth increments hovering around the 2 percent mark. When computing per capita income, therefore, an already inexact income parameter is complicated by dividing it by disparate population growth parameters. Again, assuming even that the numerator remained constant, simply the increase in the denominator — population — would most directly alter the results. This may or may not, however, set a matrix for the future, given varying age, fertility and immigration profiles among countries.

PURCHASING POWER PARITIES (PPPs)

Clearly, there are very significant problems in trying to encompass either the absolute or comparative vagaries of GDP within a common measuring framework. At least, however, in coping with variations in rates of exchange and individual costs of living, there is yet another approach — that of using purchasing power parities.[5] PPPs compare real prices in terms of how many units of local currency are needed in any specific country to buy the same amount of goods and services which one unit of currency will buy in the other country: for example, how many French francs are needed to buy in France what one U.S. dollar will buy within the United States.[6] This provides perhaps the most meaningful of

EXHIBIT 10
GDP Per Capita in Current U.S. Dollars
Using Current PPPs as a Percent of U.S. GDP

	1970	1971	1973	1975	1977	1979	1980	1981
Belgium	69	70	71	75	74	74	78	75
Canada	N.A.	—	—	—	—	—	—	—
Denmark	80	80	79	80	80	80	80	79
France	71	73	74	78	77	78	80	79
Germany	76	77	76	78	79	81	83	82
Japan	63	64	67	69	69	71	75	76
Netherlands	75	76	75	78	77	76	77	74
Sweden	N.A.	—	—	—	—	—	—	—
Switzerland	N.A.	—	—	—	—	—	—	—
United Kingdom	68	68	69	70	68	68	68	65

Source: Organization for Economic Cooperation and Development (OECD), Department of Economics and Statistics, *National Accounts: 1952-1981*, Paris, 1982.

criteria avoiding as it does most of the impact of artificial currency fluctuations and the like. And certainly, in terms of clarifying a measure of domestic well-being, it may be particularly insightful. In Exhibit 9, gross domestic product per capita in current U.S. dollars using current PPPs for the United States and selected nations from 1970 to 1981 is shown.

While unfortunately these data are not available for Sweden and Switzerland, they do indicate the still-substantial lead which the United States enjoys over the other countries for which this analysis is possible.[7] Germany, as shown in Exhibit 10, is at 82 percent of the GDP per capita of the United States, and even this exceeds Japan which is at the 76 percent mark. The data show a general comparative decline of the United States — or, perhaps phrased more positively, a comparative increase in the gross domestic product of most of the other nations detailed. The change, however, has been much more moderate than would be indicated by some of the earlier criteria which have been discussed and illustrated. This is not intended to suggest that there has not been a competitive decline in the U.S. economy, but rather to illustrate that the abruptness of this shift, and indeed its very magnitude, is deserving of much more in statistical perspective than unfortunately the purveyors of special pleading have accorded it.

In Exhibit 11, detailed data on the share of OECD's total gross domestic product by the United States, Japan, and the European Economic Community are presented, using two different criteria.[8] At the top of the exhibit, this is shown in current dollars at current exchange rates. Clearly, the various exchange rates have a very major statistical impact. Thus, the U.S. share of OECD total GDP has diminished from 1970's 47 percent to 1980's 34.37 percent, only to rebound

EXHIBIT 11
Shares of OECD Total GDP

	1970	1975	1980	1981
	GDP in Current Dollars at Current Exchange Rates			
United States	47.00	37.74	34.37	38.20
Japan	9.73	12.23	13.70	14.85
EEC*	30.35	34.26	37.06	32.23
OECD Total	100.00	100.00	100.00	100.00
	GDP in Current Dollars Using Current PPPs			
United States	38.80	37.53	37.49	37.78
Japan	12.42	13.32	14.41	14.65
EEC*	33.54	32.91	32.45	31.82
OECD	100.00	100.00	100.00	100.00

* EEC: European Economic Community

Source: Organization for Economic Cooperation and Development (OECD), Department of Economics and Statistics, *National Accounts: 1952-1981*, Paris, 1982.

to 38.20 percent in 1981. Japan shows consistent vigor, moving up by nearly half, from 9.73 percent in 1970 to 14.85 percent in 1981. Indeed, even the EEC as a whole enjoyed a very substantial increment, again through 1980, only to lose it all as a function largely of current exchange rates, by 1981.

A very different pattern emerges as the measurement is shifted to PPPs. The United States' share has barely moved in the 11-year period under consideration, as the effect of the over-inflated value of the dollar in 1970, and the understated value circa 1979, are eliminated. (Indeed, the 1981 comparisons — exchange rates versus PPPs — are remarkably similar, suggesting that by this criterion the much discussed U.S. decline in the 1970s was an artifact of exchange rate vagaries.) Japan's growth increment is substantial, but scarcely the heroic burst earlier indicated, while the EEC, indeed, shows a shrinkage since 1970. This pattern of smoothing is replicated when analysis is undertaken on a per capita basis, as shown in Exhibit 12.

This is not to trivialize the shrinkage in U.S. share, but rather to indicate that at least by one very major functional approach, it is far less drastic than has been seen by many observers.

SUMMARY

It appears that reports of America's economic demise have been somewhat

EXHIBIT 12
Indices of GDP Per Capita
(OECD = 100)

	1970	**1975**	**1980**	**1981**
	Using Current Exchange Rates			
United States	164	131	118	131
Japan	67	82	92	99
EEC*	83	96	107	93
OECD	100	100	100	100
	Using Current PPPs			
United States	135	131	129	129
Japan	86	90	96	98
EEC*	92	92	93	92
OECD	100	100	100	100

* EEC: European Economic Community

Source: Organization for Economic Cooperation and Development (OECD), Department of Economics and Statistics, *National Accounts: 1952-1981*, Paris, 1982.

exaggerated. The vagaries of assessing income, particularly in an international comparative framework, are substantial.

1. Gross domestic product (GDP) per capita, which provides a gauge of a nation's domestic income generation standardized for population size, is a basic measure for international income comparisons.
2. While this barometer generally is effective in assessing a public's economic wherewithal, conversions to a common currency standard and corrections for inflation present difficulties in international comparisons.
3. The latter are handled in different ways and produce disparate results when used to evaluate the relative economic well-being of the populations of different nations. When the GDP per capita for the United States and 10 major industrial nations are compared over the 1969 to 1981 period, under different currency conversions and price assumptions, the following pictures of economic reality result.
   a. When GDP per capita is converted to dollars at fixed 1975 exchange rates and not standardized for inflation (current prices), a significant relative diminution of the economic well-being of the United States is indicated. Ranked second only to Switzerland in 1969, it had fallen to fifth place by 1981.

b. When GDP per capita is converted to dollars at fixed 1975 exchange rates, and constant 1975 price levels are employed, the long-term decline of the economic posture of the U.S. is again pictured. However, there were substantial repositionings of all nations, as the effects of inflation were mitigated.

c. When GDP per capita at current prices and current exchange rates is used as the comparative measure, a third pattern of results is evident. (The use of current exchange rates ostensibly limits the need for direct inflation correction, since changes in exchange rates are to some degree a function of relative rates of inflation.) While a secular U.S. decline is again indicated through 1979, a major reversal since the latter date is strongly suggested.

4. Much of the comparative decline variously indicated by these alternatives results from the behavior of exchange rates and currency adjustments. Prior to 1971, the dollar was grossly overvalued as a result of fixed exchange rates. This caused the measures of U.S. economic stature to be unrealistically high. By 1979, the dollar was grossly undervalued resulting in unrealistically low measures. Analysis of relative economic positioning over the 1969–1979 period can be severely distorted by the vagaries of currency.

5. The use of purchasing power parities (PPPs) helps to cope with the variations in rates of currency exchange and costs of living. When comparative GDP per capita in current U.S. dollars using current PPPs is employed, the economic position of the U.S. is portrayed quite differently. While the U.S. has seen some relative decline over time, it is much less than that suggested by the preceding criteria; and the PPPs indicate the U.S. still has a substantial lead in GDP per capita.[9]

NOTES

1. The Organization for Economic Cooperation and Development (OECD) comprises the following nations:

Canada	Iceland
United States	Ireland*
Japan	Italy*
Australia	Luxembourg*
New Zealand	Netherlands*
	Norway
Austria	Portugal
Belgium*	Spain
Denmark*	Sweden
Finland	Switzerland
France*	Turkey
Germany*	United Kingdom*
Greece*	Yugoslavia

Asterisked are the ten member nations of the European Economic Community (EEC), or the Common Market. Only ten nations are used in the main analysis due to space limitations.

2. The following changes in consumer prices are linked to the basic patterns revealed in Exhibits 1 and 2:

Changes in Consumer Prices:
Average Annual Percent Change

	1970-75	1975-80	1979-80	1980-81
United States	6.8	8.9	13.5	10.4
Belgium	8.4	6.4	6.7	7.6
Canada	7.3	8.8	10.2	12.4
Denmark	9.3	10.4	12.3	11.7
France	8.9	10.4	13.3	13.3
Germany	6.1	4.1	5.5	5.9
Japan	11.7	6.6	8.0	4.9
Netherlands	8.7	6.0	6.5	6.8
Sweden	8.0	10.5	13.7	12.1
Switzerland	7.7	2.4	4.0	6.5
United Kingdom	13.2	14.4	18.0	11.9

Source: International Monetary Fund, Washington, D.C., *International Financial Statistics*, Monthly.

From 1970 through 1975, the U.S. had the smallest average annual gain in consumer prices, with the exception of Germany. Thus the growth in nominal U.S. GDP was restrained; in the post-1975 period, this situation clearly changed.

3. "Bretton Woods" has become a common economic reference to the landmark meeting of wartime leaders in Bretton Woods, New Hampshire in 1944, that created fixed exchange rates among major currencies. A major foundation of the system was an American guarantee to convert dollars into gold at $35 an ounce. In 1971, the agreement lapsed when the U.S. terminated dollar-to-gold conversions.

4. OECD, National Accounts: 1952-1981, Paris, 1982, p. 93. The pioneering work cited by OECD in making this conclusion includes: Milton Gilbert and Irving Kravis, *An International Comparison of National Products and the Purchasing Power of Currencies*, OEEC, 1954, and Milton Gilbert and Associates, *Comparative National Products and Price Levels*, OEEC, 1958. More recently, see: Irving B. Kravis, Alan Heston, and Robert Summers, *World Product and Income: International Comparisons of Real Gross Product*, Produced by the Statistical Office of the United Nations and The World Bank, Johns Hopkins University Press, Baltimore, 1982.

5. "The use of purchasing power parities instead of exchange rates is intended to achieve this objective. It must be emphasized, however, that this in no way implies that the purchasing power parities used here can be interpreted as norms or equilibrium levels to which exchange rates may be expected to gravitate. Firstly, the purchasing power parities used here cover the entire range of goods and services produced within countries as distinct from the very much smaller set which are traded internationally. Secondly, there are many other factors besides purchasing power parities which contribute to the determination of equilibrium levels of exchange rates — movements of capital, interest rates, etc." Ibid. p. 94.

6. "The methodology underlying the data . . . is to construct volume measures directly by revaluing the goods and services sold in different countries at a common set of international prices, in much the same way that volume measures over time within a single country can be compiled by utilizing a set of constant prices. By dividing the ratio of the GDPs of two countries expressed in their own national currencies by the corresponding ratio calculated at constant international prices, it is possible to derive the implied purchasing power parity, or PPP, between the two currencies concerned. These parities are essentially similar to the implicit price deflators derived from current and constant price

data in national accounts. PPPs are therefore international price indices linking the price levels of different countries. Ibid. p. 94.

7. The OECD tabulations relying on PPPs include only the EEC and selected other countries.

8. The balance of OECD is not listed in the exhibit; therefore the three subareas detailed — the U.S., Japan and the EEC — will not add to 100.

9. For a recent survey of methodologies, see Robin Marris, "Comparing the Incomes of Nations," *Journal of Economic Literature*, March, 1984, Vol. XXII, No. 1, pp. 40-58.

Chapter Three

PERSONAL AND FAMILY INCOME: DESPAIR OR ELATION?

In the preceding chapter, we looked at broad international comparative statistics of national income. Depending upon the criteria that are employed, a case can be made that the relative income position of the United States has deteriorated, improved or remained stable in comparison to other major industrial societies. A similar dilemma emerges when we attempt to discern the improvement or erosion over time of the real dollar income of America's individuals and households. The latter are the true cutting edge of a market-oriented society. Their profiles of expenditures, savings, and indeed much of their broad patterns of general behavior are shaped and directed by the realities of personal income, both in the absolute and in terms of trendline.

But the conventional measures of the economic well-being of Americans again paint strikingly different portraits. The average worker's weekly earnings, adjusted for inflation, declined by over 13 percent between 1973 and 1982, according to the U.S. Department of Labor. Similarly, the median family income in America, adjusted for inflation, declined by 10.5 percent from 1973 to 1982. As reported by the Bureau of the Census (U.S. Department of Commerce), real median family incomes in America (defined in terms of constant 1982 dollars) fell to $23,433 in 1982 from the 1973 peak of $26,175, a decline of $2,742 in nine years.

These pronouncements of widespread income deterioration over the past decade stand in sharp contrast to another prominent government statistic: personal income per capita. As published by the Bureau of Economic Analysis (of the U.S. Department of Commerce), inflation-adjusted per capita personal income in America grew substantially between 1973 and 1982, from $9,795 to $11,071.

Again measured in constant 1982 dollars, this represents a nine-year gain of $1,276 — or 13.0 percent — in the personal income accruing to each American.

Thus our major income benchmarks appear to be in conflict. Why is this the case? The purpose of this chapter is to attempt to answer this question, so as to provide a firmer base of understanding for subsequent analyses, most of which employ statistics emanating from these critical data bases.

In the material which follows, we will be examining, first, total personal income and aggregate household income over time. These are the larger pools of money which per capita personal income and median family income are associated with, respectively. (A detailed discussion of average weekly earnings is reserved for Chapter 6.) We then turn to a brief examination of the alternative inflation correction factors which are commonly used and whose product is key to the bulk of economic analysis undertaken by marketers and economists as well. After the inflation-adjusted aggregates are presented, the chapter closes with an analysis of the gap between median family income and per capita personal income.

TOTAL PERSONAL INCOME

Total personal income is derived within the national income and product accounts of the United States — a summation reflecting the entire complex of the nation's economic income and output and the interaction of its major components — produced by the Bureau of Economic Analysis of the U.S. Department of Commerce. Personal income is the current income received by all persons from all sources minus their personal contributions for social insurance. It includes such elements as wages and salaries, the incomes of proprietors, dividends, personal interest income and transfer payments. Also included are certain nonmonetary types of income, such as net rental value to owner-occupants of their homes and the value of services furnished without payment of financial intermediaries and food and fuel produced and consumed on farms. (The relationship of gross national product, national income and personal income is presented in Appendix A, along with changes in the distribution of personal income.)

As shown in Exhibit 1, total personal income in America has grown substantially — at least in nominal terms — in the period from 1967 to 1982. Over the 15 years, total personal income (in current dollars) more than quadrupled, from $630 billion in 1967 to over $2.5 trillion in 1982. And it is upon this base that a key variable of economic analysis — per capita personal income — is derived.

Completely distinct from total personal income — which is based upon macro-scale data — are the data presented in the aggregate household income column in Exhibit 1. Technically termed aggregate money income (or consumer income), the data represent the results of field surveys generated during the course of the Census Bureau's Current Population Survey (CPS). These in turn are pyramided to represent the nation. In each of the surveys, enumerators interview representative samples of the population with respect to income received during the previous year. (The CPS is thus concerned with a different aspect of the nation's economy: the distribution of money income to families and individuals.) The sources of income include the following: wages and salary, self-employment income, social security, pensions, government transfer payments, dividends, interest and unemployment benefits, among others. *Nonmonetary types of income are not included.*

As shown in Exhibit 1, aggregate household income (in current dollars) has also quadrupled over the 15-year period, from $485.8 billion in 1967 to over $2 trillion by 1982. However, the absolute household income for each of the respective years is considerably less than the personal income total. As noted in the far right of the exhibit, the relationship between these two measures of national prosperity has remained relatively constant over time, at or slightly below the .8 mark, i.e., for every dollar of total personal income determined by the Bureau of Economic Analysis, there is roughly $.80 of money income tallied by the aggregate responses to the Census Bureau's Current Population Survey.

It is not surprising that a gap exists between the respective totals since there is a basic definitional difference between the two data series (principally non-

EXHIBIT 1
Total Personal Income and Aggregate Household Income, U.S. Total: 1967 to 1982
(In Billions of Current Dollars)

Year	Total Personal Income	Aggregate Household Income	Ratio of Aggregate Household to Personal Income
1967	$ 630.0	$ 485.8	.771
1970	811.1	647.8	.800
1973	1,065.2	849.3	.797
1980	2,160.4	1,734.9	.803
1981	2,415.8	1,903.3	.788
1982	2,569.9	2,040.0	.794

Sources: For personal income: U.S. Department of Commerce, Bureau of Economic Analysis, *Survey of Current Business*, Volume 62, Number 7, July 1982, and *The National Income and Product Accounts of the United States, 1929-76: Statistical Tables*, 1981.

For household income: U.S. Bureau of the Census, Current Population Reports, Series P-60, No. 137, *Money Income of Households, Families, and Persons in the United States: 1981*, U.S. Government Printing Office, Washington, D.C. 1983, and earlier annual editions. U.S. Bureau of the Census, Current Population Reports, Series P-60, No. 140, *Money Income and Poverty Status of Families and Persons in the United States: 1982*, U.S. Government Printing Office, Washington, D.C., July 1983, and earlier annual editions.

EXHIBIT 2
Alternate Inflation Indices: 1967 to 1982

Year	Personal Consumption Expenditures Implicit Price Deflator*	Consumer Price Index†
1967	.814	55.1
1970	.925	64.1
1973	1.057	73.3
1980	1.792	136.0
1981	1.945	150.1
1982	2.060	159.3
1967-1973	29.8%	33.0%
1973-1982	94.9	117.3

*1972=1.00
†1977=100

Sources: For personal income: U.S. Department of Commerce, Bureau of Economic Analysis, *Survey of Current Business*, Volume 62, Number 7, July 1982, and *The National Income and Product Accounts of the United States, 1929-76: Statistical Tables*, 1981.

For household income: U.S. Bureau of the Census, Current Population Reports, Series P-60, No. 137, *Money Income of Households, Families, and Persons in the United States: 1981*, U.S. Government Printing Office, Washington, D.C., 1983, and earlier annual editions. U.S. Bureau of the Census, Current Population Reports, Series P-60, No. 140, *Money Income and Poverty Status of Families and Persons in the United States: 1982*, U.S. Government Printing Office, Washington, D.C., July 1983, and earlier annual editions.

monetary income considerations). Equally or more important, however, is the underreporting of income that is associated with household surveys. Certainly, the Census Bureau is cognizant of the problem and estimates that household income is underreported by approximately 11 percent. Nonetheless, the relative consistency of the gap over time between aggregate household income and total personal income suggests that the disparate trend between their key products, respectively per capita personal income and median family income, is not attributable to definitional differences and underreporting but rather varying approaches in accounting for inflation.

STANDARDIZING FOR INFLATION

Analyzing income statistics over time can prove misleading unless distortions caused by inflation are removed. Complicating the picture is the fact that each of the published income series, i.e., total personal income and aggregate household

EXHIBIT 3
Constant Dollar Personal and Aggregate Household Income, U.S. Total: 1967 to 1982
(In Billions of Constant 1982 Dollars)

Year	Total Personal Income	Aggregate Household Income
1967	$1,594.3	$1,404.5
1970	1,806.3	1,609.9
1973	2,076.0	1,845.8
1980	2,483.5	2,032.1
1981	2,558.6	2,020.0
1982	2,569.9	2,040.0

Intraperiod Changes

	Change		
	Number	**Percent**	**Annual Change**
Personal Income			
1967-1973	$481.7	30.2	$80.3
1973-1982	493.9	23.8	54.9
Aggregate Household Income			
1967-1973	$441.3	31.4	$73.6
1973-1982	194.2	10.5	21.6

Sources: For personal income: U.S. Department of Commerce, Bureau of Economic Analysis, *Survey of Current Business*, Volume 62, Number 7, July 1982, and *The National Income and Product Accounts of the United States, 1929-76: Statistical Tables*, 1981.

For household income: U.S. Bureau of the Census, Current Population Reports, Series P-60, No. 137, *Money Income of Households, Families, and Persons in the United States: 1981*, U.S. Government Printing Office, Washington, D.C., 1983, and earlier annual editions. U.S. Bureau of the Census, Current Population Reports, Series P-60, No. 140, *Money Income and Poverty Status of Families and Persons in the United States: 1982*, U.S. Government Printing Office, Washington, D.C., July 1983, and earlier annual editions.

income, accounts for inflation somewhat differently. The Bureau of Economic Analysis employs what is known as *GNP implicit price deflators* to correct for inflation in the National Income and Product Accounts. These measure both price shifts and changing consumption patterns. In contrast, the Census Bureau uses the *Consumer Price Index* to inflation adjust its money income series. The Consumer Price Index (CPI) is based upon a fixed market basket (i.e., a fixed consumption pattern), individual elements of which are measured in terms of prices by periodic surveys conducted under the aegis of the Bureau of Labor Statistics. Until 1983, the chief criticism of the CPI has been its heavy weighting of housing ownership. While this has now been altered the results still are mirrored in the historical data and much of the analysis upon which it has been based.

At this stage it is important to note that the rival approaches yield significantly different results. This is illustrated in Exhibits 2 and 3. The first of these presents the two inflationary indices from 1967 to 1982. During the first six years of that period, from 1967 to 1973, there was roughly a 10 percent gap; the personal consumption expenditure implicit price deflator rose by slightly under 30 percent — the CPI by 33 percent. Between 1973 and 1982, however, the gap widened substantially, with the increases respectively at the 94.9 percent mark and 117.3 percent level.

When these in turn are applied to the data shown in Exhibit 1, they yield total personal income in constant dollars — based on the implicit price deflator discussed above — and aggregate household income similarly refined, but by its own index, the CPI (Exhibit 3). The two series begin to diverge markedly as efforts are made to state them in a constant dollar format. Again, from 1967 to 1973 the gap was relatively small. Both personal income and aggregate household income grew by roughly 30 percent. From 1973 to 1982, the differences between the two widened precipitously, with personal income growing by 23.8 percent and aggregate household income by only 10.5 percent.

Why was there this substantial deviation? In very large part, it derives from the different methods for measuring inflation. The Consumer Price Index as noted above was much more sensitive to increases in homeownership costs — and these soared in the latter part of the 1970s. The implicit price deflator, on the other hand, has a strong commodity weighting — and this tended to produce a different picture of inflation. Numerous volumes and endless essays have been written both comparing and dissecting the virtues and demerits of the two indices. Nonetheless, the vision of reality of the 1973 to 1982 period is strongly conditioned by our perception of what happened to "real" income levels. If the personal income criterion is utilized — there is a respectable growth of nearly a quarter (23.8 percent). If aggregate household income is used, however, it is a comparatively minor 10.5 percent. It should be noted here that both measures have significant elements of logic and in part simplicity, as well as coverage, to commend them. The issue is not their formal reconciliation, but rather to keep their differences — and their consequences — firmly in mind as we view the data which evolve from their separate bases.

MEDIAN FAMILY INCOME AND PER CAPITA PERSONAL INCOME

Common among the measures of societal well-being which are associated with

EXHIBIT 4
Median Family Income and per Capita Personal Income, U.S. Total: 1960 to 1982
(In Constant 1982 Dollars)

Year	Median Family Income	Per Capita Personal Income
1960	$18,317	$5,633
1970	24,528	8,808
1973	26,175	9,795
1980	24,626	10,909
1981	23,761	11,131
1982	23,433	11,071

Interperiod Changes

Period	Change: Number	Change: Percent	Average Annual Change
Median Family Income			
1960-1970	$6,211	33.9	$621
1970-1973	1,647	6.7	549
1973-1982	–2,742	–10.5	–305
Per Capita Personal Income			
1960-1970	$3,175	56.4	$318
1970-1973	987	11.2	329
1973-1982	1,276	13.0	142

Sources: For personal income: U.S. Department of Commerce, Bureau of Economic Analysis, *Survey of Current Business*, Volume 62, Number 7, July 1982, and *The National Income and Product Accounts of the United States, 1929-76: Statistical Tables*, 1981.

For household income: U.S. Bureau of the Census, Current Population Reports, Series P-60, No. 137, *Money Income of Households, Families, and Persons in the United States: 1981*, U.S. Government Printing Office, Washington, D.C., 1983, and earlier annual editions. U.S. Bureau of the Census, Current Population Reports, Series P-60, No. 140, *Money Income and Poverty Status of Families and Persons in the United States: 1982*, U.S. Government Printing Office, Washington, D.C., July 1983, and earlier annual editions.

these data series are median family income and per capita personal income. The former provides the mid-point in the array of individual family incomes. The latter represents the total personal income divided by the size of the population. While they are two different measures, one would have expected that their basic patterns of change over time would coincide. But even inflation standardizing

EXHIBIT 5
Population and Labor Force Change, U.S. Total: 1960-1981
(Numbers in millions)

	Total Resident Population (April 1)	Civilian Labor Force (Annual Average)
1960	179.3	69.6
1970	203.3	82.8
1980	226.5	106.9
1981	229.3*	108.7

Intraperiod Changes

	Change	
	Number	**Percent**
Population		
1960-1970	24.0	13.4
1970-1981	26.0	12.8
Labor Force		
1960-1970	13.2	19.0
1970-1981	25.9	31.3

*July 1

Source: U.S. Department of Labor, Bureau of Labor Statistics, *Monthly Labor Review*, monthly.

procedures alone introduce significant variations. Other factors also are at work. These will be reviewed after a fuller presentation of the median family income and per capita personal trends is made.

As shown in Exhibit 4, median family income, after moving up from its 1960 base of $18,317 to a high of $26,175 in 1973, diminished subsequently to little more than $23,000 by 1982. Per capita personal income, on the other hand, showed a continous growth through 1981 — with a small decline during recession-plagued 1982. Thus, as shown in the bottom of the exhibit, the 1973-1982 pattern of median family income is one of decline — at a 10.5 percent rate. Per capita personal income in that same time frame actually increased by 13.0 percent. The former measure shows a degeneration in the well-being of America; the latter suggests the reverse.

This stands in sharp contrast to the 1960 to 1970 period, an era preceding the onslaught of harsh inflation. Over this decade, median family income increased by 33.9 percent while per capita personal income grew by 56.4 percent. With both showing vigorous growth, their differential seemed less significant. The issue then was not whether things were getting better, but how much better.

Now the question is somewhat more complex. While per capita personal income still grew during the 1973 to 1982 period, its average annual growth during the latter years ($142) was only half that ($318) of the 1960 to 1970 period (Exhibit 4). The question is not whether improvement has diminished — it clearly has — but rather whether we have slipped into absolute decline — as indicated by the median family income parameter.

THE DEMOGRAPHIC FACTOR

As earlier described, one of the reasons for this lack of clarity lies in the differing ways of correcting for inflation in the two data series. Of equal importance, however, are demographic factors. Key among the latter is a basic trendline of more workers per capita in America — over the past decade the proportion of the total population in the labor force has increased substantially. From April 1, 1970, through mid-year 1981, the total population of the United States increased by 26.0 million people, or 12.8 percent (Exhibit 5). In a perhaps unique statistical mirror image, the labor force increased by nearly precisely the same number — 25.9 million people — or 31.3 percent. The baby boom generation moved into adulthood, and the labor force participation rate moved from 60.4 percent to 63.9 percent. Over this period then — as we examine personal income per capita — the greater number of labor force participants per capita in America tended to proportionately increase the numerator (total personal income) faster than the denominator (population). This stands in marked contrast to the 1960s (Exhibit 5), when the population growth — 24 million persons — was almost twice that of the labor force gains — 13.2 million persons.

But the real growth that was achieved in per capita personal income between 1970 and 1981 ($2,323) was far less than that secured between 1960 and 1970 ($3,175), despite the fact of a proportionally greater number of persons directly contributing to income growth during the 1970 to 1981 period. A substantially greater work effort was required to achieve a smaller income gain.

Withal, the reduction in the dependency ratio, i.e., the proportion of people not in the labor force, was consequential; and despite the vagaries of unemployment, in part accounts for the relative increments in per capita incomes. The maturation of the baby boom and the advent of the baby bust generation (the decline in the number of births) gave greater prominence to the working age sector of U.S. population.

The size of the American household, however, and family as well, was shrinking quite markedly over the same decade. And perhaps the very affluence on a per capita base of American society permitted a rate of household and family formation which not only thinned out the size of family but also altered its income patterns.

Also significant is the changing configuration and composition of American families, with single parent formats representing the dominant growth sector. In terms of income, this has tended to mute the impact of the heralded "dual income" couples within the overall median family income statistics. So complex is the latter phenomenon as to be worthy of a much fuller description, which is incorporated in the following chapters.

SUMMARY

The conventional measures of the economic well-being of America's individuals and households provide conflicting pictures of income events over the past decade. Two prominent governmental statistics exemplify the dilemma.

1. As reported by the Bureau of the Census, real median family incomes (defined in constant 1982 dollars) fell to $23,433 in 1982 from a 1973 peak of $26,175, a decline of $2,742 (−10.5 percent) in nine years.
2. For the corresponding time interval, the Bureau of Economic Analysis indicates that the inflation adjusted per capita personal income grew by $1,276 (13.0 percent), from $9,795 in 1973 to $11,071 in 1982.
3. Both of these indicators are widely employed as critical economic barometers. What are the principal factors which produce such dissimilar messages? Despite definitional and measurement differences, the aggregate income pools which these individual measures (in whole or part) summarize — total personal income and aggregate household income — exhibit the same growth pattern over time in nominal (not corrected for inflation) dollars.
4. But when they are standardized for inflation, the growth patterns of the two pools diverge markedly in the post-1973 period. Total personal income grew by 23.8 percent while aggregate household income increased by only 10.5 percent (between 1973 and 1982).
5. This differential is a consequence of the reporting agencies choosing different measures to correct for inflation. The Bureau of Economic Analysis uses GNP implicit price deflators while the Census Bureau uses the Consumer Price Index (CPI). While the two indices agreed on the scope of inflation from 1967 to 1973, they varied substantially in the 1973 to 1982 period. The CPI indicated a much higher rate of inflation, thereby producing a lower rate of real income growth.
6. The per capita personal income and median family income measures, secured from these sources, suggest patterns of divergence in excess of that generated by inflation adjustments alone. Several demographic factors are thus at work.

   a. There is a basic trend of more workers per capita in America. During the last decade (1970 to 1981), absolute labor force growth was virtually identical in magnitude (25.9 million people) to the overall population growth increment (26.0 million).
   b. This has served to bolster personal income per capita, since the growing number of labor force participants per capita tended to proportionally increase the numerator (total personal income) of this statistic faster than the denominator.
   c. Concurrently, the changing configuration of American families and households, in general, tended to mute overall median family income growth.
7. These factors enable us to rationalize the differences between the two measures but do not suggest which, if either, is the more appropriate tool. This dilemma has always existed. But in periods of more sustained economic growth — 1960 to 1970, for example — the issue was not whether things were getting better, but how much better. The question now is not whether income improvement has diminished — it clearly has — but rather have we slipped into absolute decline.
8. The latter question can be explored via fuller consideration of the changing demographic and work patterns of families. Preliminary to this task is a review of the broader environment of families: households.

Chapter Four

HOUSEHOLD AND FAMILY INCOME

One of the leitmotifs of our time, to be gathered at the practically random turning of a newspaper page, is the recognition of the basic demographic trends in America. Prominent among them is the decline of the traditional family household, and the rising presence of nonmodular household types. In the analyses which follow, we have brought together in brief format some of the basic data which address both the incidence of these two household configurations as well as their relevant income statistics. The purpose of this chapter is to provide an overview of household income, which is the broader universe from which family income — as well as a whole variety of marketing generalizations — is drawn. The household examinations lend some preliminary demographic explanation to the lagging median family income benchmark, underscore the general use of the latter as a basic statistical indicator, and set the stage for more detailed analyses of family income trends in America.

AGGREGATE HOUSEHOLD INCOME BY FAMILY STATUS

In the last chapter, comparisons were undertaken of total personal income and its relationship to aggregate household income. Here our focus is on the two major household partitions: family and nonfamily. (Family households comprise two or more related individuals; nonfamily households include single person formats and arrangements encompassing two or more unrelated individuals. While families are typically viewed as married couple configurations, other arrangements are possible; a divorced father and child, for example, are considered

EXHIBIT 1
Aggregate Household Income by Family Status
U.S. Total: 1967 to 1982
(In Billions of Current Dollars)

	Total	**Family Households**	**Nonfamily Households**
1967	$ 485.8	$ 441.0	$ 44.8
1970	647.8	580.0	67.8
1973	849.3	749.9	99.4
1980	1,734.9	1,445.8	289.1
1981	1,903.3	1,576.6	326.7
1982	2,040.0	1,681.6	358.4
Intraperiod Change			
1967-1973	74.8%	70.0%	121.8%
1973-1982	140.2	124.2	260.6
Share of Total Income			
1967	100.0%	90.8%	9.2%
1970	100.0	89.5	10.5
1973	100.0	88.3	11.7
1980	100.0	83.3	16.7
1981	100.0	82.8	17.2
1982	100.0	82.4	17.6

Source: U.S. Bureau of the Census, Current Population Reports, Series P-60, No. 137, *Money Income of Households, Families, and Persons in the United States: 1981*, U.S. Government Printing Office, Washington, D.C., 1983, and earlier annual editions. U.S. Bureau of the Census, Current Population Reports, Series P-60, No. 140, *Money Income and Poverty Status of Families and Persons in the United States: 1982*, U.S. Government Printing Office, Washington, D.C., 1983, and earlier annual editions.

a family household.) Exhibit 1 provides data for selected years from 1967 through 1982 on trends in aggregate household income, further prorated between these two groups. As is evident, it is the nonfamily household whose share of aggregate income has been growing most rapidly. From 1967 to 1973, for example, family household income increased by 70 percent (in current dollars); nonfamily household income grew by more than one and a half times that rate — 121.8 percent. This disparity expanded even more markedly in the following nine years through 1982. During this period, aggregate family income grew by 124.2 percent, while nonfamily income increased by more than twice that rate — 260.6 percent.

But despite these different growth rates, family income is still by far the more important of the two subsets. Its share of total had been reduced from 90.8 per-

EXHIBIT 2
Total Number of Households by Family Status
U.S. Total: 1967 to 1982
(Numbers in thousands)
(As of March of the following year)

	Total	Family Households	Nonfamily Households
1967	60,813	50,111	10,702
1970	64,778	52,227	12,551
1973	69,859	55,053	14,806
1980	82,368	60,309	22,059
1981	83,527	61,019	22,508
1982	83,918	61,393	22,525
1967-1973	14.9%	9.9%	38.3%
1973-1982	20.1	11.5	52.1

Source: U.S. Bureau of the Census, Current Population Reports, Series P-60, No. 137, *Money Income of Households, Families, and Persons in the United States: 1981*, U.S. Government Printing Office, Washington, D.C., 1983, and earlier annual editions. U.S. Bureau of the Census, Current Population Reports, Series P-60, No. 140, *Money Income and Poverty Status of Families and Persons in the United States: 1982*, U.S. Government Printing Office, Washington, D.C., 1983, and earlier annual editions.

cent in 1967 to 82.4 percent by 1982, but its absolute magnitude in the latter year was still nearly five times that of nonfamily households. While the fashionability of nontraditional shared living arrangements has blossomed, and the sheer number of single households — both among the elderly and among youth — has increased significantly, the sum of these phenomena still represent a much smaller market target than the classic modular household of yore, i.e., \$358.4 billion versus \$1.68 trillion. Nonetheless the scale of nonfamily aggregate income is substantial. If the latter's share of total household income had remained at the 1967 level (9.2 percent), it would have been roughly \$170 billion less than was the case in 1982.

The Component Factors

The dynamics of the data presented in Exhibit 1 are a composite of two elements. The first of these, illustrated in Exhibit 2, is the shift in total number of households by family status. Family households, from 1967 to 1982, grew by some 23 percent. Nonfamily households over the same period more than doubled, from 10.7 million in 1967 to 22.5 million in 1982. Thus nonfamily households, on a base barely a fifth that of family households, had the same absolute

EXHIBIT 3
Mean Household Income by Family Status
U.S. Total: 1967 to 1982
(In Current Dollars)

	Total	Family Households	Nonfamily Households
1967	$ 7,989	$ 8,801	$ 4,186
1970	10,001	11,106	5,402
1973	12,157	13,622	6,713
1980	21,063	23,974	13,106
1981	22,787	25,838	14,515
1982	24,309	27,391	15,911
1967-1973			
Number	$ 4,168	$ 4,821	$ 2,527
Percent	52.2%	54.8%	60.3%
1973-1982			
Number	$ 12,152	$13,769	$ 9,198
Percent	100.0%	101.1%	137.0%

Source: U.S. Bureau of the Census, Current Population Reports, Series P-60, No. 137, *Money Income of Households, Families, and Persons in the United States: 1981*, U.S. Government Printing Office, Washington, D.C., 1983, and earlier annual editions. U.S. Bureau of the Census, Current Population Reports, Series P-60, No. 140, *Money Income and Poverty Status of Families and Persons in the United States: 1982*, U.S. Government Printing Office, Washington, D.C., 1983, and earlier annual editions.

increment of growth — approximately 11 million — in the 15-year period under discussion.

The second element in accounting for the total household income variance is the absolute level of income secured by each of the household types. In Exhibit 3, mean data by family status is shown. While mean nonfamily household income has grown from less than half that of family households in 1967 to nearly 60 percent by 1982, the absolute gap between the two has widened. If a marketing manager focused just on the mean absolute dollar increments available to each household type, the potential targets are still substantially at variance: family households in the eight-year period from 1973 to 1982 secured an income gain of more than $13,700, while nonfamily household gained barely $9,000.

In sum, therefore, the aggregate household income data shown in Exhibit 1 (where the nonfamily income total increased twice as fast as that of families between 1973 and 1982) is the product of far greater rates of growth in nonfamily household numbers (five times faster than family households — Exhibit 2) and

EXHIBIT 4
Median Household and Median Family Income
U.S. Total: 1967 to 1982
(In Current and Constant 1982 Dollars)

	Median Household Income		**Median Family Income**	
	Current Dollars	**Constant 1982 Dollars**	**Current Dollars**	**Constant 1982 Dollars**
1967	$ 7,143	$20,651	$ 7,933	$22,935
1970	8,734	21,712	9,867	24,528
1973	10,512	22,832	12,051	26,175
1980	17,710	20,745	21,023	24,626
1981	19,074	20,244	22,388	23,761
1982	20,171	20,171	23,433	23,433

Intraperiod Change
(Constant 1982 Dollars)

	Change	
	Number	**Percent**
Median Household Income		
1967-1973	$ 2,181	10.6
1973-1982	–2,661	–11.7
Median Family Income		
1967-1973	$ 3,240	14.1
1973-1982	–2,742	–10.5

Source: U.S. Bureau of the Census, Current Population Reports, Series P-60, No. 137, *Money Income of Households, Families, and Persons in the United States: 1981*, U.S. Government Printing Office, Washington, D.C., 1983, and earlier annual editions. U.S. Bureau of the Census, Current Population Reports, Series P-60, No. 140, *Money Income and Poverty Status of Families and Persons in the United States: 1982*, U.S. Government Printing Office, Washington, D.C., 1983, and earlier annual editions.

smaller absolute increments of mean nonfamily income growth (two-thirds that of mean family income growth — Exhibit 3).

When the trends in household income (mean or median) are used casually either as an indictment of slow growth in America or for any other purpose, it must be kept in mind that they are substantially the product not merely of national economic trends, but even more importantly of demographic variations, with the

EXHIBIT 5
U.S. Households by Size, Total Number and Median Household Income: 1975 to 1982
(Households as of March the following year; total numbers in thousands)

Household Totals

Size of Household	1975	1982	Change: 1975 to 1982 Number	Percent
Total	72,867	83,918	11,051	15.2
1 person	14,983	19,250	4,267	28.5
2 persons	22,321	26,439	4,118	18.4
3 persons	12,520	14,793	2,273	18.2
4 persons	11,407	13,303	1,896	16.6
5 persons	6,268	6,105	– 163	– 2.6
6 persons	3,001	2,460	– 541	–18.0
7 persons or more	2,367	1,568	– 799	–33.8

Median Household Income
(In Current Dollars)

Size of Household	1975	1982	Number	Percent
Total	$11,800	$20,171	8,371	70.9
1 person	4,806	9,984	5,178	107.7
2 persons	11,171	20,201	9,030	80.8
3 persons	14,083	24,445	10,362	73.6
4 persons	15,849	27,617	11,768	74.3
5 persons	16,489	27,176	10,687	64.8
6 persons	16,142	27,191	11,049	68.4
7 persons or more	14,623	23,717	9,094	62.2

Source: U.S. Bureau of the Census, Current Population Reports, Series P-60, No. 137, *Money Income of Households, Families, and Persons in the United States: 1981*, U.S. Government Printing Office, Washington, D.C., 1983, and earlier annual editions. U.S. Bureau of the Census, Current Population Reports, Series P-60, No. 140, *Money Income and Poverty Status of Families and Persons in the United States: 1982*, U.S. Government Printing Office, Washington, D.C., 1983, and earlier annual editions.

share of nonfamily configurations — and their relatively low incomes — expanding.

The total number of households therefore increases and is somewhat adulterated in terms of income characteristics because of the high share of relatively low income configurations which have been added over time.

EXHIBIT 6
U.S. Households by Age, Total Number and Median Household Income: 1975 and 1982
(Households as of March the following year; total numbers in thousands)

Age of Householder	1975	1982	Change: 1975 to 1982 Number	Change: 1975 to 1982 Percent
	Household Totals			
Total	72,867	83,918	11,051	15.2
15 to 24 years*	5,877	5,695	−182	−3.1
25 to 34 years	15,510	19,104	3,594	23.2
35 to 44 years	12,227	16,020	3,793	31.0
45 to 54 years	12,820	12,354	−466	−3.6
55 to 64 years	11,631	13,074	1,443	12.4
65 years and over	14,802	17,671	2,869	19.4
	Median Household Income (In Current Dollars)			
Total	$11,800	$20,171	$ 8,371	70.9
15 to 24 years*	8,138	13,816	5,678	69.8
25 to 34 years	13,127	21,281	8,154	62.1
35 to 44 years	15,542	6,370	10,828	69.7
45 to 54 years	16,322	27,985	11,663	71.5
55 to 64 years	12,485	22,075	9,590	76.8
65 years and over	5,585	11,041	5,456	97.7

*14 to 24 years in 1975.

Source: U.S. Bureau of the Census, Current Population Reports, Series P-60, No. 137, *Money Income of Households, Families, and Persons in the United States: 1981*, U.S. Government Printing Office, Washington, D.C., 1983, and earlier annual editions. U.S. Bureau of the Census, Current Population Reports, Series P-60, No. 140, *Money Income and Poverty Status of Families and Persons in the United States: 1982*, U.S. Government Printing Office, Washington, D.C., 1983, and earlier annual editions.

RELATING MEDIAN HOUSEHOLD AND MEDIAN FAMILY INCOMES

This is illustrated in Exhibit 4 which provides data on median household income for all households versus that for families alone. As is evident in the exhibit, the latter provides a somewhat more salubrious picture. When appraised in constant 1982 dollars, for example, median household income actually declined between 1967 and 1982 ($20,651 to $20,171). Median family income on the other hand has increased, although relatively slightly ($22,935 in 1967 to $23,433 in 1982). Thus using the family partition provides a much more positive view of the U.S.'s economic performance than does the broad household equivalent.

When the 15-year period is partitioned using the year 1973, the internal dynamics again become even more apparent; median household income increased by 10.6 percent from 1967 to 1973, while median family income grew by 14.1 percent. Similarly, while median household income has declined by 11.7 percent between 1973 and 1982, median family income has contracted by a more moderate 10.5 percent rate. Clearly, though families as such have done better in terms of income than holds true for households in total, neither of them can point to a positive statistical picture in more recent years. Here again, however, the data require some measure of demographic analysis in order to clarify the full measure of the dynamics which are at work.

EXPLAINING THE PATTERN OF HOUSEHOLD INCOME

While discussion of the internal vagaries of family income will be reserved for the next chapter, so much stress has been placed upon the relative failure of real median household income to show growth over time as to make it worthy of additional study. Exhibits 5 and 6 illustrate some of the configurational changes over time which are central to the overall phenomenon. Illustrated in Exhibit 5 is the change both in number and in median income of households, classified by size (the number of persons which they contain). The data are presented both for 1975 and 1982. The top of the exhibit forcefully illustrates the shrinking scale of household configurations in America. While the total number of households grew by one in seven (15.2 percent), one person households grew by nearly three in ten (28.5 percent), far outpacing any other configuration. At the other end of the size spectrum, there was an absolute decline in the number of households with five or more persons, with the extreme cases — those with seven persons or more — shrinking by a third (33.8 percent) in the seven-year period under discussion. Of the total growth of 11.1 million households from 1975 to 1982, 4.3 million were single person configurations, while an additional 4.1 million comprised two person formats.

The significance of this growth pattern becomes apparent when we focus on the bottom of Exhibit 5, where median household income is shown for each of the size categories discussed above. It is one and two person configurations — which accounted for over 75 percent of the 1975 to 1982 growth increment — that by far have the lowest median incomes of any of the household sizes illustrated. The median income of one person households in 1982, for example, only approached $10,000, less than half of the median for all households and barely a third of that of four, five, or six person households. And even the $20,200 median income of two person configurations was comparatively small when viewed in the context of the mid $27,000 range which characterized households with four to six persons.

The product of these shifts was one which severely influenced the overall image of household income. Small, relatively low-income households grew much more rapidly in number than larger more affluent ones. It is the shift in internal configuration, the size of household, which more forcefully explains the household income data.

But is this not merely a sophistry — are smaller households simply poorer households or does the capacity to promulgate smaller households indicate in some measure the sheer wealth of society? A poor society simply cannot afford individual shelter arrangements for even three and four person households much less one and two persons. In our opinion a strong case can be made that in a perverse fashion, the phenomenon of household fragmentation, even though it helps precipitate a decline in the median household income (for all households), by some measure is a gauge of affluence rather than its reverse.

U.S. HOUSEHOLDS BY AGE

In part, the shrinking size of household illustrated in Exhibit 5 is a reflection of the shifting age profile of America's households, which is detailed in Exhibit 6. The reverberations of the later stages of the baby boom between 1975 and 1982 have left as the largest single cohort households headed by individuals from 25 to 34 years of age (Exhibit 6). When income data by age are examined, it is evident that this group, at least by historical precedents, is approximately 20 years from its premier earning years. For example, the median income for this cohort is presently at the $21,000 mark. For the cohort currently 35 to 44 years of age, the median income exceeds $26,000. At the top of the income ladder stand those in the 45- to 54-year-old age bracket, whose median income exceeds $27,900. It is noticeable that it is this very same group — born during the low fertility period of the Depression — which has shrunk in absolute number in the six-year period under discussion. In part, therefore, the shrinkage of real household incomes is accounted for by the comparative age configurations of those very same households — with age and income closely linked. The importance of the elderly (65 years and over) in this sphere should not be overlooked: their 19.4 percent increase in number clearly weights down the overall median, since their income is barely half that of all households.

SUMMARY

Measuring income in America is a complex task. Simple generalizations are highly dubious in this arena. Changes in America's demographic profile are significant in altering the distribution of aggregate income across the array of household types. In general, the changes have tended to dampen growth as gauged by measures of individual household or family well-being.

1. The share of aggregate household income accruing to nonfamily household configurations increased from 9.2 percent in 1967 to 17.6 percent in 1982.
2. While the scale of nonfamily income is substantial, and while the fashionability of nontraditional and shared living arrangements has blossomed — as has that of single occupancies — the aggregate income pool is still dominated by family configurations: $1.7 trillion versus $358.4 billion in 1982.
3. This continued dominance is a consequence of the much lower incomes attached to the rapidly proliferating nonfamily household types.
    a. Nonfamily households increased five times as fast as family configurations during the 1973 to 1982 period. Their absolute gain of almost 8 million (from 14.8 million in 1973 to 22.5 million in 1982) was one-third higher than the 6 million gain experienced by family households (from 55.1 million in 1973 to 61.4 million in 1982).
    b. But the income disparities were substantial. In 1982, mean nonfamily income stood at $15,911, far below that of family arrangements ($27,391). And even though the former grew at a faster rate than the latter, the absolute gap between the two still widened over the past decade.
    c. The product of these two phenomena is an absolute income share captured by nonfamily households which — while growing — does not match the scale of their increased numerical presence in American society.
4. Two detailed demographic partitions — size of household and age of householder — help explain the lag in income among nonfamily households.
    a. The fastest growing size configurations comprise one and two persons. Their median income levels, however, fall far below that of all households.
    b. The categories declining in absolute numbers, those with five or more persons, have income levels far above that of all households.
    c. Households with householders 25 to 34 years old — the baby boom generation — experienced the greatest absolute growth. However, their median income was far below that of households in their premier earning years (45 to 54 years of age) — the Depression era progency; the latter actually declined in number, reflecting the sharp decline in the birth rate during the late 1920s and 1930s.
    d. And the ranks of the elderly, with quite modest incomes, also had substantial absolute growth.
5. Thus unique demographic alterations in America during the decade of the

1970s partly account for the lagging central measures of income tendencies (mean and median) since 1973.

6. Within this context, the family partition provides more continuity over time, though far from static in configuration. It is to a fuller examination of the demographic and income profile of families that we now turn.

Chapter Five

FAMILY INCOME: POST-AFFLUENCE OR DEMOGRAPHIC DISTORTIONS?

Rarely questioned in the two- and one-half decades following World War II was the promise in America not only of a high standard of living, but an always rising standard of living. This presumption began to be challenged during the 1970s by the faltering of general income patterns. As presented in Chapter 3, both total personal income and aggregate household money income showed diminished growth in the post-1973 period (despite different inflation-correcting procedures). And median family income at the same time gave evidence not only of a slower rise in the standard of living, but a fundamental redirection toward a less-affluent society.[1]

This transformation directly coincided with the 1973 and 1979 energy shocks; in each of the two-year periods following these events, real median family incomes experienced sharp reversals. By 1982, the American family's economic wherewithal, as gauged by median family income, was roughly equivalent to that in 1968.

The potential distortions induced by using the Consumer Price Index to standardize for inflation were discussed in Chapter 3, while the preceding chapter began the exploration of the influence of household demographics. This chapter will continue to evaluate the latter in terms of the major family partitions. Are there unique short-term family demographics which have distorted our indices, or has the nation's income producing capacity been fundamentally altered?

AFFLUENCE AND STAGNATION

The years of American world economic hegemony and post-World War II affluence were highlighted in the 1969 comparisons of international income

EXHIBIT 1
Median Family Income: 1950 to 1982

Year	Actual Dollars	Constant 1982 Dollars
1950	$ 3,319	$13,318
1960	5,620	18,317
1970	9,867	24,528
1971	10,285	24,513
1972	11,116	25,648
1973	12,051	26,175
1974	12,902	25,254
1975	13,719	24,604
1976	14,958	25,363
1977	16,009	25,500
1978	17,640	26,099
1979	19,661	26,047
1980	21,023	24,626
1981	22,388	23,761
1982	23,433	23,433

Gains in Real Income
(Constant 1982 Dollars)

Period	Number	Percent	Average Annual Gain
1950-1960	$ 4,999	37.5	$ 500
1960-1970	6,211	33.9	621
1970-1973	1,647	6.7	549
1973-1982	–2,742	–10.5	–305

Source: U.S. Bureau of the Census, Current Population Reports, Series P-60, No. 140, *Money Income and Poverty Status of Families and Persons in the United States: 1982 (Advance Data from the March 1983 Current Population Survey)*, U.S. Government Printing Office, Washington, D.C., 1983.

(Chapter 2). They are even more accentuated when the long-term distribution of income to families is reviewed. As shown in Exhibit 1, real median family income gains of almost $5,000 (in constant 1982 dollars) were secured in the decade of the 1950s and over $6,200 in the decade of the 1960s. Thus the median family income in America increased from $13,318 in 1950 to $24,528 by 1970, a virtual doubling in real terms.

But the escalator faltered after median family income peaked in 1973 ($26,175). Indeed, despite tentative upward thrusts in the ensuing years — the second oil shock in 1979 coincided with the end of renewed income growth —

the median family income in 1982 fell to $23,433, well below the 1973 high. The $2,742 real income loss over the 1973 to 1982 period is a sad reminder of the achievements of the previous two decades.

The critical dilemma of American society is whether the nadir of 1982 is a recession by-product, or a new reality of stagnation. The cyclical nature of the pattern is strongly emphasized via close examination of the post-1973 constant dollar column of Exhibit 1. The peak income year, 1973, coincided with the business cycle peak. The recessionary trough, 1975, marked the termination of a two-year median income descent. Recovery and expansion, 1975 through 1979, had as its parallel the resumption of income growth to a level just below the 1973 pre-oil embargo threshold.

EXHIBIT 2
Upper Income Families: 1960 to 1982
Constant 1982 Dollars
(Families as of March of the following year)
(Numbers in thousands)

	1960	1973	1982
TOTAL FAMILIES	45,539	55,053	61,393
Income $25,000 and over			
Number*	12,796	28,903	28,486
Percent	28.1	52.5	46.4
Income $50,000 and over			
Number*	N.A.	6,331	6,691
Percent	N.A.	11.5	10.9

*Derived from published percent distribution.

Source: U.S. Bureau of the Census, Current Population Reports, Series P-60, No. 140, *Money Income and Poverty Status of Families and Persons in the United States: 1982 (Advance Data from the March 1983 Current Population Survey)*, U.S. Government Printing Office, Washington, D.C., 1983.

After the economy was buffetted by the second oil shock of 1979, a second income slide was experienced. A much more severe recessionary pattern ensued — 1980 and 1981-82 — with an anti-inflationary monetarist policy exacerbating the aftermath of the energy crunch. As a result, the income slide bottomed out as the recession ended officially in November, 1982.

As of this writing, the recovery and expansion phases of the business cycle — roughly corresponding to 1983 and 1984, respectively — should be paralleled by

EXHIBIT 3
Family Distribution: 1960 to 1982
Constant 1982 Dollars
(Families as of March of the following year)
(Numbers in thousands)

	1960	1973	1982
Total Families	45,539	55,053	61,393
less than $5,000	4,190	2,092	3,684
$5,000 to $14,999	13,070	10,900	14,182
$15,000 to $24,999	15,483	13,158	15,041
$25,000 to $34,999 }		15,085	11,971
$35,000 to $49,999 }	12,796	7,487	9,823
$50,000 and over }		6,331	6,692
Proportional Share (percent)			
Total Families	100.0	100.0	100.0
less than $5,000	9.2	3.8	6.0
$5,000 to $14,999	28.7	19.8	23.1
$15,000 to $24,999	34.0	23.9	24.5
$25,000 to $34,999 }		27.4	19.5
$35,000 to $49,999 }	28.1	13.6	16.0
$50,000 and over }		11.5	10.9

Source: U.S. Bureau of the Census, Current Population Reports, Series P-60, No. 140, *Money Income and Poverty Status of Families and Persons in the United States: 1982 (Advance Data from the March 1983 Current Population Survey)*, U.S. Government Printing Office, Washington, D.C., 1983.

the resumption of growth in median family income. If this proves to be solidly the case, it is possible to view the pattern of the past decade as the result of unique ''shocks,'' absorbed by the system.

THE UPPER INCOME STRATA

Much attention has been focussed on the new ''upscale'' market in America — a growing elite whose sustained consumption patterns appear immune to the difficulties buffetting the average family. But when data on upper income families are reviewed (in constant 1982 dollars) via broad income partitions over the past decade, it is difficult to segment myth from reality (Exhibit 2). In 1960, for example, only 12.8 million out of 45.5 million families (28.1 percent) had incomes of $25,000 and over. By 1973 that proportion had almost doubled, reaching a peak of 52.5 percent; in that year, 28.9 million out of 55.1 million families reached this base. But by 1982, despite the total number of families increasing to 61.4 million, the ''aspiring affluent'' actually declined in absolute (28.5 million) and relative importance (46.4 percent). Indeed, if we review the proportion of families with incomes of $50,000 and over (once again stated in constant 1982 dollars), they comprised 11.5 percent of all families in 1973; by 1982, their proportion had declined to 10.9 percent (although their absolute number expanded).

Again this analysis, by tracing the broad pattern from business cycle peak (1973) to recession (1982) obscures the intraperiod dynamics. This concern will be addressed more fully after another broad generalization is reviewed — the fading of the American Middle Class.

IS THE MIDDLE CLASS DISAPPEARING?

Further perspective on distributional patterns can be secured from Exhibit 3, where the brackets are narrowed across the overall income profile. Focusing on the upper end ($25,000 and over) of the spectrum, in absolute terms there has been a ''thinning out'' of the $25,000 to $34,999 category (from 15.1 million to 12.0 million households) between 1973 and 1982, a ''thickening-up'' of the $35,000 to $49,999 sector (from 7.4 million to 9.8 million households) and absolute, but small, expansion in the $50,000 and over group (from 6.3 million to 6.7 million). Concurrently, the income categories under $25,000 expanded in absolute terms, with the greatest numerical (and proportional) gains registered in the under $15,000 classification.

Repartitioning the data again, there was strong growth in the number of families with incomes under $15,000 between 1973 and 1982, shrinkage in the $15,000 to $34,999 sector, and growth at the upper end — $35,000 and over. While far from definitive evidence, what the data suggest is the fragmentation of the vast monolithic middle market. Certainly, the almost obsessive retail focus on the ''upscale'' market would suggest that this is the case. Does this reflect a fundamental restructuring of the American economy and governmental policy? Or are there demographic forces which have exerted considerable influence? These are compelling questions, but their urgency may be lessened as we shift our measurement baselines.

When the peaks and troughs of the business cycle are emphasized, the pattern appears to represent a much more cyclical phenomenon:

	(Peak) 1973	**(Recession) 1975**	**(Peak) 1979**	**(Recession) 1982**
Total	100.0%	100.0%	100.0%	100.0%
Less than $15,000	23.6	26.3	25.1	29.1
$15,000-$34,999	51.3	51.2	43.9	44.0
$35,000 and over	25.1	22.4	30.9	26.9

EXHIBIT 4
Families by Age of Householder, Total Number and Median Family Income: 1975 and 1982
(Households as of March of the following year; total numbers in thousands)

	Family Totals		Change: 1975 to 1982	
Age of Householder	**1975**	**1982**	**Number**	**Percent**
Total	56,245	61,393	5,148	9.2
15 to 24 years*	4,042	3,436	- 606	-15.0
25 to 34 years	12,885	14,217	1,332	10.3
35 to 44 years	11,107	13,658	2,551	23.0
45 to 54 years	11,125	10,476	- 649	- 5.8
55 to 64 years	8,923	10,009	1,086	12.2
65 years and over	8,163	9,597	1,434	17.6
	Median Family Income (In Current Dollars)			
Total	$13,719	$23,433	$9,714	70.8
15 to 24 years*	8,752	14,266	5,514	63.0
25 to 34 years	13,659	22,286	8,627	63.2
35 to 44 years	15,921	27,480	11,559	72.6
45 to 54 years	17,569	30,727	13,158	74.5
55 to 64 years	14,869	26,122	11,253	75.7
65 years and over	8,057	16,118	8,061	100.0

*14 to 24 years in 1975

Source: U.S. Bureau of the Census, Current Population Reports, Series P-60, No. 140, *Money Income and Poverty Status of Families and Persons in the United States: 1982 (Advance Data from the March 1983 Current Population Survey)*, U.S. Government Printing Office, Washington, D.C., 1983.

During recessionary years (1975 and 1982), there is a strong tendency for the lower-income bracket to expand relative to the preceding business cycle peaks (1973 and 1979), respectively. The converse is true — shrinkage — in the $35,000 and over income category.

When we examine either peak to peak (1973 to 1979) or recession to recession (1975 to 1982) trendlines, there is indeed some middle-class shrinkage in proportional terms. But the result is much more a thickening-up of the upscale market ($35,000+) than expansion in the lower-income sector. Invoking generalizations without adequate attention to baselines and recessionary distortions can lead

EXHIBIT 5

Families by Type, Total and Median Family Income: 1975 and 1981

(Families as of March the following year)

(Numbers in thousands)

			Change: 1975 to 1981				Change: 1975 to 1981	
	1975*	1981†	Number	Percent	1975	1981	Number	Percent
Total	56,245	61,019	4,775	8.5	$13,719	$22,388	8,669	63.2
Married Couple Families	47,318	49,630	2,312	4.9	14,867	25,065	10,198	68.6
Wife in paid labor force	20,833	25,002	4,169	20.0	17,237	29,247	12,010	69.7
Wife Employed	19,334	23,237	3,903	20.2	17,584	29,866	12,282	69.8
Full Time	13,512	15,911	2,399	17.8	18,262	31,161	12,899	70.6
Part Time	5,821	7,326	1,505	25.9	16,223	27,068	10,845	66.8
Wife Unemployed	1,499	1,765	266	17.7	13,260	21,097	7,837	59.1
Wife not in paid labor force	26,486	24,628	-1,858	-7.0	12,752	20,325	7,573	59.4
Male Householder‡	1,444	1,986	542	37.5	12,995	19,889	6,894	53.1
Female Householder‡	7,482	9,403	1,921	25.7	6,844	10,960	4,116	60.4

*Householder 14 years old and over.

†Householder 15 years old and over.

‡Spouse absent.

Source: U.S. Bureau of the Census, Current Population Reports, Series P-60, No. 137, *Money Income of Households, Families and Persons in the United States: 1981*, U.S. Government Printing Office, Washington, D.C., 1983; and previous annual editions for the respective years.

to misleading assertions. This was particularly the case in the early 1980s since the 1982 recession marked the worst downturn since the Great Depression.

Nonetheless, major demographic forces still exerted pressure throughout the period. They will be analyzed in the balance of the chapter. After viewing the shifting age structure of American families, their changing configurational and working patterns will be examined, paying particular attention to the wide variations in income which are evident across these partitions.

FAMILY AGE STRUCTURE

The elderly and the baby boom generation have been the dominant forces impacting the changing age structure of American families (Exhibit 4). Virtually all of the growth that occurred between 1975 and 1982 was accounted for by families whose householders were 65 years and older and between 25 and 44 years of age. And large portions of these age clusters had incomes lagging the overall medians (both the elderly and the 25 to 34 years of age segments). Thus a rise in many young family formations — distant in time from their peak earning years; sustained absolute growth in the number of elderly families — long past their prime income years; and a decline in the size of the 45 to 54 years of age sector — a group in their premier earning period, all served to mute the pattern of family income growth in America.

CHANGING CONFIGURATIONS

But simple age data tend to cloak both the forces of family work force expansion and the process of family fragmentation that occurred simultaneously over the past decade. The reality that the good life in America increasingly requires a household economic team of two workers is well recognized. But its positive impact has been countered by the rise of nonmarried couple families, which served as a stubborn offset to overall income growth.

Exhibit 5 provides detailing on changes both in number and in income (in current dollars) of family configurations between 1975 and 1981.[2] While families in total increased by 8.5 percent (4.8 million), married couple families increased by only 4.9 percent (2.3 million) over this period. This latter increment was the result of a 4.2 million increase (20.0 percent) in married couples with wives in the paid labor force and a 1.9 million shrinkage (−7.0 percent) in married couple families with wives not in the labor force. And the major gains were achieved in full time employment (2.4 million or 17.8 percent) rather than part time status (1.5 million or 25.9 percent).

Equally significant is the overall magnitude of the increase in married couple families with wives employed (3.9 million) in comparison to that of non-married couple families (2.5 million) — male or female householders, no wife or hus-

EXHIBIT 6
Families by Type and Householder Working Year-Round Full Time
Median Family Income: 1981
(In Current Dollars)

	All Families	**Husband and Wife Year-Round Full-Time Workers**
Total	$22,388	$28,680
Married Couple Families	25,065	30,222
Wife in Paid Labor Force	29,247	32,224
Wife Employed	29,866	32,606
Full Time	31,161	33,956
Part Time	27,068	30,025
Wife Unemployed	21,097	25,090
Wife Not in Paid Labor Force	20,325	26,581
Male Householder*	19,889	25,059
Female Householder*	10,960	16,795

*Spouse absent

Source: U.S. Bureau of the Census, Current Population Reports, Series P-60, No. 137, *Money Income of Households, Families and Persons in the United States: 1981*, U.S. Government Printing Office, Washington, D.C., 1983.

band present (Exhibit 5) — the configurations with lower income potentials.[3] But while the absolute growth of single parent families (2.5 million) was only half that of married couples with wives employed, it was actually greater than the numerical increase in all married couple families (2.3 million). And in terms of rates of growth, male and female householders (single parent families) grew eight and five times faster, respectively, than married couple families.

The wide income variation as a function of family configuration and the employment status of wives is also shown in Exhibit 5. At the upper rungs of the income ladder in 1981 were married couple families with wives employed full time. Their median of $31,161 (in current dollars) contrasts sharply with the overall median family income of $22,388. The penalty of wives not in the labor force ($20,325) or of single parent status (male householder, $19,889 — female householder, $10,960) is substantial.

Thus the nominal median family income gain of $8,669 from 1975 to 1981 (virtual stagnation in constant dollars) was facilitated via the addition of almost 4 million employed wives. But the substantial increase in work effort was counterbalanced by the addition of 2.5 million single parent families, 1.9 million of

EXHIBIT 7
All Married Couple (Husband-Wife) Families and Husband and Wife Both Year-Round Full-Time Workers: 1975 to 1981
(Families as of March of the following year)

	All Married Couple (Husband-Wife) Families	Husband and Wife Year-Round Full-Time Workers	
		Number	Percent
1975	47,318	7,385	15.6
1976	47,497	7,730	16.3
1977	47,385	8,130	17.2
1978	47,692	8,959	18.8
1979	48,180	9,308	19.3
1980	49,294	9,360	19.0
1981	49,630	9,627	19.4

Source: U.S. Bureau of the Census, Current Population Reports, Series P-60, No. 137, *Money Income of Households, Families and Persons in the United States: 1981*, U.S. Government Printing Office, Washington, D.C., 1983; and previous annual editions for the respective years.

them female householders. With a 1981 median income less than half that of all families, the latter served as an effective depressant within the total family income profile.

Again, the ability to spawn single spouse families may indicate in some measure the affluence of American society, while at the same time precipitating a decline in overall median family income. In the case of divorce, for example, a relatively middle income married couple family with children may fragment into two of the least resource-endowed household formats — a single parent family (with the spouse who secures child custody) and a single person household — both of whose median income parameters hover in the vicinity of $10,000. The very widespread availability of shelter resources has permitted the scale of such phenomena.

THE NEW WORKER ELITE

With more than half of all married couple families having wives in the labor force in 1981, the often evoked image is of surging numbers of two worker families failing to keep pace on the income treadmill. Reality, however, is far more complex.

EXHIBIT 8
All Married Couple Families and Wife Employed Full Time, Householder Year-Round Full-Time Workers: 1975 to 1981
Median Income
(In Current Dollars)

Year	Married Couple Families	Wife Employed Full-Time Householder Year-Round Full-Time Worker
1975	$14,867	$20,185
1976	16,203	21,387
1977	17,616	23,045
1978	19,340	25,377
1979	21,503	28,189
1980	23,141	31,099
1981	25,065	33,956

Source: U.S. Bureau of the Census, Current Population Reports, Series P-60, No. 137, *Money Income of Households, Families and Persons in the United States: 1981*, U.S. Government Printing Office, Washington, D.C., 1983; and previous annual editions for the respective years.

The data in Exhibit 5 did not offer any insights into the work activities and labor force status of husbands. In this context, the partitioning presented in Exhibit 6 proves illuminating. In the first column, the 1981 median income levels by family type are again presented; in the second column, a subset of the first is isolated — those families whose householder (predominantly the husband) is also a year-round full-time worker.[4] For total families (all configurations), the latter subset has a median income ($28,680), over $6,000 greater than that of all families. This differential, to greater or lesser extent, is apparent through the entire family profile, yielding a much more sanguine vision of present family income realities.

The growth of wives in the labor force also produces another fallacious image: that 50 percent of all husband-wife families have two *full-time* workers. Accepting the latter interpretation would make even more ominous the median family income performance over the past decade. But only 19.4 percent of all married couple families had both the husband and wife working year-round full time in 1981 (Exhibit 7). While up sharply from 15.6 percent in 1975, it is far from the commonly promulgated "half" of all married couple families. Thus there is a very substantial reservoir of potential income additions — four out of five married couple families — which could serve to bolster the median statistics. Nonetheless, the addition of almost 2.3 million dual income married couples

EXHIBIT 9
Median Family Income: 1981 Householder Year-Round, Full-Time Worker, Wife Employed Full Time
(Families as of March 1982)

	Income
Total	$33,956
Householder Age	
18-24 Years	22,933
25-34	30,939
35-44	35,570
45-54	39,036
55-64	36,318

Source: U.S. Bureau of the Census, Current Population Reports, Series P-60, No. 137, *Money Income of Households, Families and Persons in the United States: 1981*, U.S. Government Printing Office, Washington, D.C., 1983.

(both working full time, year-round), only permitted overall family income stabilization (in constant dollars) in the 1975 to 1981 period, since this increment was offset by the absolute growth in single parent families.

The income levels of the new "elite" are shown in Exhibit 8. Not only are there income "premiums" accompanying husband-wife full-time employment status ($33,956 in 1981) — versus all married couple families ($25,065) — there is also a "bonus" as a function of age (Exhibit 9). Capturing the highest median income are married couple families whose head is between 45 and 54 years of age — and both of whose principals are employed full time year-round. The households that meet these requirements have a median income in excess of $39,000 per year. Above and below that age group incomes are significantly lower.

It is this demographic age-related income premium which may portend brighter market opportunities to come — the potential of the huge maturing baby boom cohort replicating the age-related income experience depicted in Exhibit 9. Whether such a vision is realizable, however, is strongly dependent on the growth potential of the American economy for the balance of the decade.

SUMMARY

Attempts to depict the overall economic well-being of American families via single income statistics is a formidable task. The changing pool of families over time, shifts in demographic composition and emerging work force patterns converge and interact with more than a little turbulence. These phenomena are often obscured by dependence on a simple summary measure of overall median family income.

1. The overall median family income in the United States fell by more than $2,700 in inflation-corrected 1982 dollars between 1973 and 1982. This followed a 23-year period when real median family incomes virtually doubled.
2. This was paralleled by an absolute decline in the 1973 to 1982 period in the number of families enjoying the perquisites of middle class status (incomes $25,000 and over in constant 1982 dollars). In the previous 13 years (1960 to 1973), there had been a more than doubling in the number of families attaining this income threshold.
3. Further analysis of income distributions over time suggests some fragmentation in the vast middle market of America — growth in the extremes (the number of families with incomes under $15,000 and $35,000 and over) and shrinkage in the middle ($15,000 to $34,999).
4. Underpinning these changes have been complex demographic forces. The changing age structure of American families is important in this context. Substantial growth in the number of young family formations — distant in time from their peak earning years; sustained absolute growth in the number of elderly families — long past their prime income years; and a decline in size of the 45 to 54 years of age sector — a group in their premier earning period: all served to mute median family income growth.
5. Two other counterbalancing demographic forces were at work: the dynamics of family work force expansion and the process of family dissolution.
    a. While married couple families increased by only 4.9 percent (2.3 million) between 1975 and 1981, married couples with wives employed increased by 20.2 percent (3.9 million), with 2.4 million of the latter employed full time.
    b. Concurrently, single parent families (male and female householders, spouse absent) increased by 27.6 percent (2.5 million); their absolute growth increment exceeded that of all married couple families.
    c. These family subsets have vastly different income realities. The 1981 median income of married couple families with wives employed full time — $31,161 (in current dollars) — far exceeded the overall median family income of $22,388. In contrast, the 1981 median income of female householders (spouse absent) barely exceeded $10,000.
    d. Thus while a vastly increased volume of work bolstered overall median family incomes, the rise of single parent families concurrently served as an effective depressant.

NOTES

1. This statement assumes, of course, that the Consumer Price Index serves as an adequate tool for standardizing for inflation.

2. The 1981 data are the latest available tabulations, at this writing, detailing employment status of wives and multiple worker families.

3. For ease of expression, we will also designate non-married couple families (i.e., male and female householders, spouse absent) as single parent families, although other living arrangements fall under this classification.

4. Prior to 1980, the husband in a married couple family was always considered to be the "householder" or "head of household." Beginning in 1980, either the husband or wife was listed as householder, with the former still predominating.

5. For example, the labor force participation rate of males 55 to 64 years of age was 89.6 percent in 1947. By 1980, it had fallen to 72.3 percent.

Chapter Six

EMPLOYMENT, EARNINGS AND INCOME

In the preceding chapters, patterns of income variation have been explored via alternative definitions both internationally and domestically and, in the case of the latter, across an array of demographic partitions. The purpose of this chapter is to examine one of the major income bulwarks — wages and salaries (or earnings) — and its association with the basic income parameters that have been presented for the past two decades.

This apparently simple task, however, has many complexities: earnings vary sharply by industrial sector, the very nature of the industrial structure is shifting markedly (and is subject also to short-term dislocations caused by the vagaries of the business cycle), and earnings account for a changing portion of total income. The untangling of the precise cause-effect linkages are well beyond the scope of the book; nonetheless, specific patterns and associations present themselves with such clarity that given their importance, a general overview is warranted.

CHANGES IN AMERICA'S EMPLOYMENT STRUCTURE

In order to secure perspective on the changes in the income of Americans, it is essential to fully observe the enormous potency of the shifts that are taking place in what Americans do to make a living. The issues of what is noise and what is message, what is transient versus the longer-lasting driving forces of the economy, are far from resolved. But over and above all of the impacts of the business cycle are the crucial shifts that are taking place within the employment structure of the United States.

EXHIBIT 1
U.S. Nonfarm Payroll Employment: 1960 to 1982*
(Numbers in thousands)

	Total Employment	Goods Producing	Service Producing
1960	54,189	20,434	33,755
1970	70,880	23,578	47,302
1973	76,790	24,893	51,897
1980	90,406	25,658	64,748
1982	89,630	23,882	65,748

Intraperiod Changes

	Change	
	Number	Percent
Total Employment		
1960-1970	16,691	30.8
1970-1973	5,910	8.3
1973-1982	12,840	16.7
(1970-1982)	(18,750)	(26.5)
Goods Producing		
1960-1970	3,144	15.4
1970-1973	1,315	5.6
1973-1982	-1,011	-4.1
(1970-1982)	(304)	(1.3)
Service Producing		
1960-1970	13,547	40.1
1970-1973	4,595	9.7
1973-1982	13,851	26.7
(1970-1982)	(18,446)	(40.0)

*Excludes self-employed and unpaid family workers.

Source: U.S. Department of Labor, Bureau of Labor Statistics, *Employment and Earnings*, monthly.

The broad parameters of change are shown in Exhibit 1. From 1960 to 1982, total nonfarm payroll employment in the United States soared by over 35 million jobs. If, however, we focus on the goods-producing sector (i.e., mining, construction and manufacturing) of the economy, virtual stagnation is evident. In 1960, there were 20 million goods-producing jobs. The total peaked in 1980 at only 25.6 million and following the recession of 1982 had retreated back to the

EXHIBIT 2
U.S. Nonfarm Payroll Employment, by Detailed Sector: 1973 to 1982*
(Numbers in thousands)

			Change: 1973 to 1982	
	1973	1982	Number	Percent
Total	76,790	89,630	12,840	16.7
Goods Producing	24,893	23,882	−1,011	−4.1
Mining	642	1,121	479	74.6
Construction	4,097	3,913	− 184	−4.5
Manufacturing	20,154	18,848	−1,306	−6.5
Service Producing	51,897	65,748	13,851	26.7
Transportation and Public Utilities	4,656	5,058	402	8.6
Wholesale and Retail Trade	16,607	20,551	3,944	23.7
Finance, Insurance and Real Estate	4,046	5,350	1,304	32.2
Services	12,857	19,001	6,144	47.8
Government	13,732	15,788	2,056	15.0

*Excludes self-employed and unpaid family workers.

Source: U.S. Department of Labor, Bureau of Labor Statistics, *Employment and Earnings*, monthly.

same level as 1970 (23.6 million). Thus it is the service-producing sector (broadly defined) which has accounted for the vast bulk of employment growth. A near doubling from 1960 to 1982 yielded a net addition of 32 million jobs, or 90 percent of the total growth in non-farm payroll employment. The gap between the goods-producing and service-producing sectors in terms of overall job activity has widened since 1973, with the latter actually expanding, despite the recession of 1980-82, while the goods-producing sector, as earlier indicated, contracted.

The components of these broad economic segments are detailed for the 1973 to 1982 period in Exhibit 2. It is manufacturing in the goods-producing sector which has faltered most markedly, with a decline of 6.5 percent, or 1.3 million jobs, in the 9-year period under consideration. This was nearly matched in percentage terms by the decline in construction, which — like manufacturing — tends to be closely linked to the overall vigor of the economy.[1]

EXHIBIT 3
Gross Weekly Earnings (Average)
by Industry Division: 1964-1982
(In Current Dollars)

				Percent Change	
	1964	**1973**	**1982**	**1964-1973**	**1973-1982**
Total Private	$ 91	$145	$267	59.3	84.1
Goods Producing					
Mining	118	201	461	70.3	129.4
Construction	132	236	425	78.8	80.1
Manufacturing	103	166	331	61.2	99.4
Service Producing					
Transportation and Public Utilities	119	203	402	70.6	98.0
Wholesale and Retail Trade	75	112	198	49.3	76.8
Finance, Insurance and Real Estate	86	129	245	50.0	89.9
Services	70	117	225	67.1	92.3

Note: Mean earnings of production and related workers in mining and manufacturing, construction workers in construction, and nonsupervisory employees in private service-producing industries.

Source: U.S. Department of Labor, Bureau of Labor Statistics, *Employment and Earnings*, monthly.

The situation is very different as we focus on the constituents of the service-producing arena, where each of the industrial divisions has expanded. The single largest percentage and absolute gain was accounted for by services per se, which increased by more than 6 million jobs or 47.8 percent. While the service sub-sector will be explored more fully in a later section of this chapter, its explosive presence is noteworthy. By 1982, services alone accounted for more jobs in America than did manufacturing. And they were joined in this status by wholesale and retail trade, whose 20.5 million jobs in 1982 far exceeded the 18.8 million in manufacturing. Moreover, the absolute growth in finance, insurance and real estate employment from 1973 to 1982 matched the absolute decline in manufacturing. While certainly this may not represent one-for-one substitution, it is illustrative of a shifting nature of a post-industrial economy.

EXHIBIT 4
Gross Weekly Earnings (Average)
by Industry Division: 1978-1982
(Constant 1977 Dollars)

	1978	**1979**	**1980**	**1981**	**1982**
Total Private	$189	$183	$173	$170	$168
Goods Producing					
Mining	309	304	292	293	290
Construction	296	286	270	266	268
Manufacturing	232	225	212	212	208
Service Producing					
Transportation and Public Utilities	281	272	258	255	253
Wholesale and Retail Trade	143	138	130	127	125
Finance, Insurance and Real Estate	165	159	154	153	154
Services	152	146	140	139	142

Note: Mean earnings of production and related workers in mining and manufacturing, construction workers in construction, and nonsupervisory employees in private service-producing industries.

Source: U.S. Department of Labor, Bureau of Labor Statistics, *Employment and Earnings*, monthly.

THE LINKAGE OF INDUSTRIAL DIVISIONS AND EARNINGS

What do changes in employment structure mean to the earnings of Americans? The powerful relationship is illustrated in Exhibits 3 and 4, which provide, in current and constant dollars, respectively, gross average weekly earnings by industry division for selected years.[2] It is the fast-growth job sectors which have the lowest weekly earnings both historically and presently; and conversely, it is the high earnings sectors — i.e., mining, construction, and manufacturing — which involve the smallest absolute growth in jobs over time. (The only exception to this pattern is the high earnings characterizing transportation and public utilities which, as a glance back at Exhibit 2 indicates, is the smallest division of the service-producing sector.) Thus, for example, jobs circa 1982 in mining, on average, had more than twice the earnings attached to them as did services. Gross

EXHIBIT 5
Median Usual Weekly Earnings
by Age and Sex: 1973 and 1982
(In Current and Constant 1977 Dollars)

Current Dollars

			Change: 1973 to 1982	
	1973	**1982**	**Number**	**Percent**
Total, Full Time	$159	$308	$149	93.7
Men				
16 to 24 Years	136	234	98	72.1
25 and Over	203	402	199	98.0
Women				
16 to 24 Years	103	196	93	90.3
25 and Over	121	254	133	109.9

Constant 1977 Dollars

			Change: 1973 to 1982	
	1973	**1982**	**Number**	**Percent**
Total, Full Time	$217	$194	$–23	–10.6
Men				
16 to 24 Years	185	147	–38	–20.5
25 and Over	277	253	–24	– 8.7
Women				
16 to 24 Years	140	123	–17	–12.1
25 and Over	165	160	– 5	–3.0

Note: Data refer to wage and salary workers and the incorporated self-employed, who usually work full time on their sole or primary job.

Source: U.S. Department of Labor, Bureau of Labor Statistics, *Employment and Earnings*, monthly.

average weekly earnings in manufacturing were $331 while those in finance, insurance and real estate were a far more modest $245. Therefore, just as a function of changes in what Americans do for a living — weekly earnings for the *average working American* would have gone down.

While the cause-and-effect relationships are obscure — i.e., high weekly earnings industries may be those which are most vulnerable to staffing reductions

EXHIBIT 6
Civilian Labor Force, by Sex and Age, 1970 to 1982, and Projection to 1990 (Middle BLS Projection)
(Numbers in thousands)

	1970	1982	1995	Change: 1970 to 1982 Number	Change: 1970 to 1982 Percent	Change: 1982 to 1995 Number	Change: 1982 to 1995 Percent
Total, Age 16 and Over	82,771	110,204	131,387	27,433	33.1	21,183	19.2
Men, Total	51,228	62,450	69,970	11,222	21.9	7,520	12.0
16 to 24	9,725	13,074	10,573	3,349	34.4	– 2,501	–19.1
25 to 34	11,327	17,793	18,105	6,466	57.1	312	1.8
35 to 44	10,469	12,781	19,446	2,312	22.1	6,665	52.1
45 to 54	10,417	9,784	13,807	– 633	– 6.1	4,023	41.1
55 and Over	9,291	9,019	8,039	– 272	– 2.9	– 980	–10.9
Women, Total	31,543	47,755	61,417	16,212	51.4	13,662	28.6
16 to 24	8,121	11,533	10,557	3,412	42.0	– 976	– 8.5
25 to 34	5,708	13,393	16,300	7,685	134.6	2,907	21.7
35 to 44	5,968	9,651	17,427	3,683	61.7	7,776	80.6
45 to 54	6,532	7,105	11,125	573	8.8	4,020	56.5
55 and Over	5,213	6,073	6,008	860	16.5	– 65	– 1.1

Source: Howard N. Fullerton, Jr., and John Tschetter, "The 1995 Labor Force: A Second Look." *Monthly Labor Review*, Volume 106, Number 11, November 1983, p. 5.

— and are outside the parameters of this study, it is noteworthy, as we focus on the right-hand column of Exhibit 3, that it is the slow growth employment divisions which have enjoyed the highest rates of earnings growth.

This situation is further accentuated, as the data shown in Exhibit 3 are summarized for the 1978 to 1982 period in constant dollars, in Exhibit 4. It is all too evident that there has been a decline, by this measurement base, of gross weekly earnings in every industry division — and this has been a steady process since 1978, rather than merely resulting from the 1981-1982 recession.

In sum, the average weekly earnings of Americans have been impacted perhaps as much by a changing industrial structure as by the vagaries of the business cycle. Both of them, however, have combined in recent years to, at the very least, dampen — and in most cases, substantially reduce — real incomes. But there are other factors at work as well.

DEMOGRAPHICS AND EARNINGS

The changes in America's work force in terms of both age and sex variations, as the focus shifts to median usual weekly earnings, are enormously consequential.[3] In general, as shown in Exhibit 5, newcomers to the labor force, typically at the 16 to 24 years of age level, have far lower earnings than their seniors, a relationship which has continued over time. Thus, in 1982, men 16 to 24 years of age had median usual weekly earnings of $234, while those 25 years old and over had nearly double that — $402. Similarly, the case among women though less accentuated was still consequential — with the 16 to 24 year old group at $196 in 1983, and those 25 years of age and over at $254.

The 9 years from 1973 to 1982, were a peak entry-into-the-labor-force period for the baby boom generation. Further illustrating the dynamics underway are the data at the bottom of Exhibit 5, which show detailed earnings changes in constant 1977 dollars. As is brought home in these data, the shrinkage in real usual weekly earnings was much more prevalent among youth — both male and female — than those 25 years of age and over.

Was this a market phenomenon of wages for youth being driven down by the sheer size of the age cohort applying for jobs? Or rather was it a consequence of no growth in the high-paying, goods-producing sector, by very definition not in a position to take on youthful newcomers? Certainly, the changes in the civilian labor force by sex and age shown in Exhibit 6 give some support to the demographic argument. From 1970 to 1982, for example, the number of men in the labor force between 16 and 24 years of age grew by more than a third (3.3 million) with an equal absolute growth and an even larger percentage gain (42 percent) among women of an equivalent age. Thus, nearly one in four of the total additions to the labor force was in the 16 to 24 years of age entry-level sector. It is striking to note that the one area of labor force decline involved men 45 years of age and over — typically the peak earning years.

EXHIBIT 7
Gross National Product, Employment and Income

		Employment‡		
Year	**GNP***	**Manufacturing**	**Service Producing**	**Median Family Income§**
1971	$1,122	18,623	48,278	$24,513
1972	1,186	19,151	50,007	25,648
1973	1,254	20,154	51,897	26,175
1974	*1,246*	*20,007*	53,471	*25,254*
1975	*1,232*	*18,323*	54,345	*24,603*
1976	1,298	18,997	56,030	25,363
1977	1,370	19,682	58,125	25,500
1978	1,439	20,505	61,113	26,099
1979	1,479	21,040	63,363	26,047
1980	*1,474*	*20,285*	64,748	*24,626*
1981	*1,503*†	*20,173*	65,625	*23,761*
1982	*1,477*	*18,848*	65,748	*23,433*

*Gross National Product, in billions of constant 1972 dollars.
†Two negative-growth quarters during year.
‡Numbers in thousands.
§Constant 1982 dollars.

Source: U.S. Department of Commerce, Bureau of Economic Analysis, *Survey of Current Business*, monthly.

U.S. Department of Labor, Bureau of Labor Statistics, *Employment and Earnings*, monthly.

A NEW DEMOGRAPHIC FUTURE?

There are many uncertainties as we attempt to project future trends. One of the firmest sectors, though still ambiguous at the margin, is the size of the civilian labor force. In the right-hand side of Exhibit 6 changes projected by the Bureau of Labor Statistics in this vital sector from 1982 to 1995 are shown. The 13-year forecast yields a total accession to the labor force of only 21 million participants, substantially under the 27 million of the preceding 12 years. Most of this shrinkage is accounted for by men, particularly youthful men, 16 to 24 years old, who will decline by 2.5 million. The decline in women in the labor force within this age group totals nearly 976,000. Thus there is substantial shrinkage both among men and women 16 to 24 years old, i.e., the lowest earning sector; the bulk of the labor force growth is among those who traditionally have been among the highest earners, i.e., the 35-54 year old category.

The wage and salary earnings decline of the late 1970s, to the degree that it is a reflection of demographics, may well be reversed in the decade to come. But obviously, this is dependent upon the overall vigor of the economy and the opportunities that are available for a maturing labor force. Certainly, the historic linkages between an expanding economy and manufacturing are significant.

GNP, EMPLOYMENT AND INCOME

The heavy importance of manufacturing-related earnings, despite the shrinking proportion of Americans who earn their living in this sector, is evidenced in Exhibit 7. Without going into the issues of "what causes what," the powerful association between overall changes in GNP, the vigor of manufacturing employment, and median family income is readily apparent. The recession years (underlined in the exhibit), 1974-75 and then 1980-82, highlight the harshness of this relationship. Service-producing jobs have shown an amazing independence of the basic trends in GNP. From 1973 to 1975, for example, GNP fell by more than $20 billion in constant 1972 dollars. Yet service-producing employment over the same time span continued to expand by nearly 2.5 million jobs. It was manufacturing which both reflected and contributed to the decline of GNP — with a reduction of 1.8 million jobs in the same three-year period. Concurrently, median family income fell by roughly $1,500 in constant 1982 dollars.

In expansionary periods, 1975 to 1979 for example, the dynamic is reversed. GNP expansion and manufacturing employment resurgence is associated with the renewal of real median family income growth. At the same time, services experienced explosive growth. Unfortunately, the pattern again reverted during 1980 through 1982, a period of even deeper recession than the 1974-75 experience. While service employment increased by 1 million jobs, manufacturing declined by an equivalent figure. The end result was median family incomes plummeting by $1,200.

The relative modesty of wages in the service producing sector, in contrast to those in manufacturing, suggests that jobs in the former sector at present appear to be inadequate surrogates for declines in the classic "blue collar" sectors, at least as they are reflected in median family income. Will these relationships continue in the future? Or are other elements influencing the pattern shown in Exhibit 7?

EARNINGS AND INCOME

The changes in gross average weekly earnings when compared with median family income, detailed in Exhibit 8, provide some insight into this issue. Growth over time in median family income has consistently outpaced the equiv-

EXHIBIT 8
Gross Weekly Earnings (Average) and Median Family Income: 1960 to 1982
(In Current Dollars)

Year	Gross Average Weekly Earnings	Median Family Income
1960	$ 80.67	$ 5,620
1970	119.83	9,867
1973	145.39	12,051
1980	235.10	21,023
1982	266.92	23,433

Intraperiod Changes

	Change	
Average Weekly Earnings	**Number**	**Percent**
(1960-1982)	($186.25)	(230.9)
1960-1970	39.16	48.5
1970-1973	25.56	21.3
1973-1982	121.53	83.6
Median Family Income		
(1960-1982)	($17,813)	(317.0)
1960-1970	4,272	75.6
1970-1973	2,184	22.1
1973-1982	11,382	94.4

Source: U.S. Bureau of the Census, Current Population Reports, Series P-60, No. 140. *Money Income and Poverty Status of Families and Persons in the United States: 1982 (Advance Data from the March 1982 Current Population Survey)*, U.S. Government Printing Office, Washington, D.C., 1983.

U.S. Department of Labor, Bureau of Labor Statistics, *Employment and Earnings*, monthly.

alent pattern of average weekly earnings changes. As shown in the exhibit, while the gap has narrowed between the two rates of increase between the 1960 to 1970 and the 1973 to 1982 periods (a 76 percent income growth versus a 48 percent increase in average weekly earnings in the former period as against a 94 percent-84 percent differential in the latter), it is still significant. This is in part a tribute to more Americans at work within the family unit, even though this is

EXHIBIT 9
Personal Income and its Disposition
(In Billions of Current Dollars)

	Dollars			Percent		
	1960	**1973**	**1981**	**1960**	**1973**	**1981**
Total	$402	$1,065	$2,416	100.0	100.0	100.0
Wage and Salary Disbursements	272	703	1,494	67.7	66.0	61.8
Other Labor Income	11	49	140	2.7	4.6	5.8
Proprietors' Income	47	94	125	11.7	8.8	5.2
Rental Income of Persons	14	23	34	3.5	2.2	1.4
Dividends	13	27	63	3.2	2.5	2.6
Personal Interest Income	25	94	329	6.2	8.8	13.6
Transfer Payments	29	120	336	7.2	11.3	13.9
Social Insurance Contribution	− 9	−43	− 105	−2.2	−4.0	−4.3

Source: *Survey of Current Business*, Volume 62, Number 7, July 1982.

muted by lower increments in weekly earnings per worker. But to this must be added changes in the pattern of sources of personal income.

Wage and salary disbursements are declining in importance as a proportion of total personal income (Exhibit 9). In 1960, for example, wages and salaries were 67.7 percent of total personal income. By 1981, they had fallen to 61.8 percent. The most significant changes were those in personal interest income and transfer payments. In 1960, for example, transfer payments were less than one-ninth of wages and salaries. By 1981, the ratio had moved up well past the one-fifth level. Personal interest income by this later time, nearly matched the significance of transfer payments. And the sum of the two elements represented more than a quarter of total personal income by 1981.

Whether this shifting composition represents a diversion of resources which otherwise would flow into production, or whether conversely it provides a flywheel of demand for the American economy which would be lacking in recession years (or both), is heavily debated. The one definitive judgement that can be made at this stage of insight is that the changes are sizeable!

PLACING THE CHANGING PATTERNS OF U.S. EMPLOYMENT IN AN INTERNATIONAL CONTEXT

As criticism of the performance of the American economy has mounted, one

EXHIBIT 10
Total Civilian Employment in the U.S., Four Largest European Nations, and Japan: 1970 to 1982*
(Numbers in thousands)

			Change: 1970 to 1982	
	1970	**1982**	**Number**	**Percent**
United States	78,678	99,526	20,848	26.5
Four Largest European Countries, Total	89,290	88,920†	− 370	−0.4
France	20,320	20,980†	660	3.2
Germany	26,100	25,090†	−1,010	−3.9
Great Britain	23,780	22,460†	−1,320	−5.6
Italy	19,090	20,390	1,300	6.8
Japan	50,940	56,857‡	5,917	11.6

*Includes self-employed, other non-payroll, and agricultural employment.
†Preliminary.
‡Third Quarter.

Source: Janet L. Norwood, "Labor Market Contrasts: United States and Europe," *Monthly Labor Review*, Volume 106, Number 8, August 1983, pp. 3-7 (for U.S. and Europe).

OECD, *Labor Force Statistics: 1969 to 1980*, Paris, 1982, and *Quarterly Supplements* (for Japan).

of the principal measuring sticks has been comparison with the patterns that exist in other countries. All too frequently some of these have been made without appropriate awareness of variations in measurement criteria. (A glance back at Chapter 2 indicates the difficulties of international income comparisons.)

The gross parameters, however, of civilian employment in the United States as against some of the major developed nations do provide insight at least into the macro data. As illustrated in Exhibit 10, the absolute and relative growth of U.S. employment (including self-employed and family workers in addition to payroll employment) from 1970 to 1982 has little parallel in the four largest European countries, nor for that matter in Japan.[4] The total employment increase in the U.S. was very comparable to the *total* employment base of France or Italy, and barely lagged the *total* number of jobs extant in Great Britain or Germany. Indeed, while the U.S. job increase was more than a quarter (26.5 percent), the pattern was actually negative for the four largest European countries combined, which experienced a net loss of 0.4 percent. Germany and Great Britain each lost more than one million jobs over the 12-year period, with total civilian employment declining by 3.9 percent and 5.6 percent, respectively. Japan, in contrast,

EXHIBIT 11
Total Civilian Employment in the U.S., Selected European Nations, and Japan by Economic Sector: 1970 to 1982[a]
(Numbers in thousands)

Year	United States	France	Germany	Great Britain[b]	Italy	Japan
Agriculture[c]						
1970	3,567	2,821	2,262	782	3,839	8,860
1981	3,519	1,800	1,402	647	2,731	5,570
1982	3,571	(d)	1,371	(d)	2,525	(d)
Goods Producing[e]						
1970	26,080	7,917	12,465	10,531	7,586	18,190
1981	28,995	7,208	10,885	8,028[f]	7,722	19,700[g]
1982	27,070	(d)	10,480[f]	(d)	7,594	(d)
Service Producing						
1970	49,031	9,605	11,442	13,071	7,656	23,890
1981	67,883	11,968	13,261	14,373[f]	10,003	30,540
1982	68,888	(d)	13,251[f]	(d)	10,277	(d)

a. Small adjustments made to the overall employment data in Exhibit 10 could not be made to certain sectoral data. Includes self-employed, other non-payroll and agricultural employment.
b. Includes Northern Ireland.
c. Includes forestry, hunting and fishing.
d. Not available.
e. Manufacturing, mining, and construction.
f. Preliminary.
g. Includes utilities.

Source: Janet L. Norwood, "Labor Market Contrasts: United States and Europe," *Monthly Labor Review*, Volume 106, Number 8, August 1983, pp. 3-7 (for U.S. and Europe).

OECD, *Labor Force Statistics: 1969 to 1980*, Paris, 1982, and *Quarterly Supplements* (for Japan).

represents a far more salubrious picture. Its absolute employment growth approached 6 million jobs, or 11.6 percent. This rate of increase, however, is less than 40 percent of the U.S. equivalent; in absolute job growth it represents less than 30 percent of the gain of the United States. Again, these data should be compared with those in Chapter 2, which illustrate the unique demographic patterns of the United States in the 12-year period under consideration.

EXHIBIT 12
Detailed Service Employment, United States, 1973-1982, and 1982 Average Weekly Earnings
(Employment in thousands)

	1973	1982	Change: 1973 to 1982 Number	Change: 1973 to 1982 Percent	1982 Average Weekly Earnings
TOTAL SERVICES	12,857	19,001	6,144	47.8	$225
Hotels and Lodging	854	1,099	245	28.7	152
Personal Services	906	925	19	2.1	161
Business Services	1,935	3,298	1,363	70.4	228
Advertising	123	159	36	29.2	328
Credit Reporting, Collection	81	75	− 6	− 7.4	—
Mailing, Reproduction	86	132	46	53.5	—
Services to Buildings	364	533	169	46.4	152
Personnel Supply	256	558	302	118.0	—
Computer and Data Processing	120	358	238	198.3	321
Auto Repair Services and Garages	422	580	158	37.4	253
Miscellaneous Repair Services	205	294	89	43.4	310
Motion Pictures	207	212	5	2.4	238
Amusements and Recreation	535	837	302	56.4	185
Health Services	3,641	5,777	2,136	58.7	230
Offices of Physicians	498	819	321	64.5	218
Offices of Dentists	206	335	129	62.6	190
Nursing and Personal Care Facilities	659	1,066	407	61.8	152
Hospitals	2,051	3,005	954	46.5	259
Legal Services	295	566	271	91.9	300
Educational Services	975	1,181	206	21.1	—
Elementary & Secondary	239	307	68	28.5	—
Colleges & Universities	644	749	105	16.3	—
Social Services	552	1,183	631	114.3	—
Membership Organizations	1,410	1,535	125	8.9	—
Miscellaneous	684	1,061	377	55.1	394
Engineering and Architectural Services	372	569	197	53.0	433
Accounting, Auditing and Bookkeeping	214	353	139	65.0	326

Source: U.S. Department of Labor, Bureau of Labor Statistics, *Employment and Earnings*, monthly.

DETAILED SECTORS

In order to underscore these disparate growth patterns, Exhibit 11 isolates the major employment sectors of the United States and their equivalents in the set of nations cited above. The basic picture is a relatively static one in the goods-producing sectors for *all* of the countries presented here. The United States from 1970 to 1981 experienced minor growth; the several European countries collectively were stagnant, at best, while Japan's gain in goods-producing employment, though slightly larger than that of the United States, was still modest. (It should be noted that Japan includes utilities in its definition, unlike the United States.)

It is not surprising that the service-producing sector demonstrated absolute growth in all the nations detailed in Exhibit 11. What is startling are the unique level and scale of the expansion of services in the U.S. Thus while the pattern of services enlargement is international, the United States carries the flag in the procession. And, as we face a future in which labor-intensive, goods-producing employment increasingly is seen as the province of the hitherto less developed nations, it is the service sector which must compensate. To the degree that this statement has validity — the United States has progressed much further than its peers.

It is of interest to note the pattern in agriculture. The United States, with the exception of Great Britain, has the smallest proportion of its labor force involved in this sector. And the U.S. level has remained static since 1970. Again with the exception of Great Britain, the problems of agriculture displacement, as opportunities in this domain shrink, may be much more substantial for the other nations shown here.

DETAILING THE AMERICAN SERVICE SECTOR

Earlier in this Chapter (see Exhibit 2), the major employment divisions of the service-producing sector in the United States were detailed. These included transportation and public utilities; wholesale and retail trade; finance, insurance and real estate; government; and most potent of all, services per se. This latter is the fastest growing of the divisions, reflecting employment gains of fully 47.8 percent from 1973 to 1982. So important is this development as to make it worthy of further detailing, provided in Exhibit 12. We have further linked — where available — average weekly earnings for each of the service classifications (on the right side of the exhibit). By far the largest absolute employment gains are in the domain of health services (2.1 million jobs), business services (1.4 million), and social services (over 600,000).

The sheer richness and heterogeneity of the array in Exhibit 12 indicates the deepening of America's life patterns and practices. One has only to pick out the near doubling of legal services in the 12-year period under consideration, the even more substantial doubling of social services, or, within business services, the tripling of computer and data processing services and the doubling of personnel supply services, to realize the deviation from the patterns of barely a dozen years ago.

THE DILEMMAS

The state of the art is much more impressive in analyzing history than in forecasting what is to come. But even in the former province, there are substantial variations of perception. Have we gone through an era in which America willy-nilly has been losing much of its historic smokestack industry potency? Are employment increases in services by default of competitive status in the emerging world-wide economy? Or rather is the track record of the United States, particularly when compared with its principal industrial peers, one of advanced adaptation?

Arguments can be advanced that the patterns of the last dozen years, portrayed in the presentations above, represent a gap in the relatively smooth web of job-earnings-income growth which we enjoyed in the 25 years following the end of World War II — that the distortions and shortfalls were solely the consequence of transient factors enumerated in our first chapter, i.e., the oil crises and the unique demographic and social shifts characterizing the 1970s. Pursuing this logic further would suggest that with these deviants largely assimilated, the pattern of higher earnings per worker, as well as incomes, will be reinstated.

Or is the issue one of drastic structural readjustment representing an abrupt disjuncture with our historic state? The assertion has been made that America is rapidly becoming a nation of low-wage, fast-food attendants — and certainly the growth of jobs in this sector exceeds the decline in manufacturing employment.[5] While the former still represents a relatively small fraction of the activities in which Americans earn their living, the massive surge in relatively low-earnings, service-producing employment is evident.

The call for a formal industrial policy implicitly is based upon the presumption that we are not dealing with implacable trendlines, moving the nation out of old activities at the cost of premium wage levels, but rather are permitting this to happen through a failure of national direction. A glance at the data presented in Exhibit 11 on our principal competitors would raise some issue on this crucial point — all developed nations are losing jobs in smokestack industries. What can be asserted with confidence based on the historical track record is an unparalleled competence in the United States in generating new jobs — perhaps not premium ones — but levels of absolute and comparative growth in employment that have no parallel in other developed nations.

SUMMARY

The American economy is continuing its long-term evolution in the context of the peaks and troughs of the business cycle. The ramifications for employment, earnings and income are slowly emerging and will represent critical parameters bounding American society in the years to come.

1. The employment structure of the United States — what Americans do to make a living — is undergoing a long-term transformation. Total nonfarm payroll employment expanded by 35 million jobs between 1960 and 1982. But the goods-producing sector accounted for only 3 million new jobs; the service-producing sector added 32 million.
2. Within the goods-producing arena, manufacturing has markedly contracted, losing 1.3 million jobs between 1973 and 1982. In contrast, each industrial division of the broad services-producing sector has experienced substantial growth, with the services division *per se* accounting for the largest percentage and absolute gain — 6.1 million jobs or 47.8 percent.
3. The income consequences of this industrial restructuring are partially revealed by earnings' patterns. It is the fast growth job sectors which have the lowest gross average weekly earnings both historically and presently; conversely, it is the high earnings sectors — goods-producing — which involve the smallest absolute growth in jobs over time. Therefore, just as a function of changes in what Americans do for a living, average weekly earnings in America would be reduced.
4. Also serving to dampen income growth are age-related earnings differentials. For both men and women, median usual weekly earnings are far lower for full-time workers under 25 years of age than those of their more senior counterparts — 25 years old and over. And the gap has widened over time. With the last decade a peak entry-into-the-labor-force period for the baby boom generation, the demographic influence on earnings was significant.
5. The 1980s may herald a reversal of the income and earnings patterns of the 1970s, at least to the degree they are linked to demographics. The bulk of the labor force will be among those who traditionally have been the highest earners — the 35 to 54 year olds.
6. But the business cycle and manufacturing employment also will exert influence on overall earnings and income trendlines. During recessionary periods, GNP, manufacturing employment and median family incomes decline, regardless of growth in service-producing jobs. The converse is true during the upside segments of the business cycle. And these relationships have persisted through the economic swings of the past decade, despite the diminishing share of wages and salaries as a percentage of total personal income.
7. These concerns are not limited to the United States. The advanced industrial

nations of Europe, as well as Japan, have all experienced contraction/stagnation in the goods-producing-employment sectors of their economies. But only the United States has experienced explosive growth in service-producing employment.

8. The detailed service-industry components bulwarking America's employment gains of the past two decades span a wide range of heterogeneous activities. At the forefront stand legal services, social services, computer and data processing services, and personnel supply services, all of which at least doubled in employment between 1970 and 1982.

NOTES

1. By November 1983, exactly 1 year after the beginning of the recovery — the 1981-82 recession spanned the July 1981 to November 1982 period — manufacturing employment totalled 19.3 million. This represented a 1 million job gain over the 18.3 million level of November, 1982.

2. Gross average weekly earnings are determined via establishment records compiled by the Bureau of Labor Statistics; they refer to mean earnings of production and related workers in mining and manufacturing, construction workers in construction, and nonsupervisory employees in private service-producing industries.

3. Median usual weekly earnings are based on household interviews conducted by the Bureau of the Census for the Bureau of Labor Statistics. The household survey measures median earnings of wage and salary workers in both the private and public sectors. Data refer to the usual earnings received from the worker's sole or primary job.

4. Due to this broader definition, the U.S. data is not directly comparable to that presented in Exhibits 1 and 2, which are limited to nonfarm payroll employment.

5. The "eating and drinking places" subset of retail trade grew from 3.1 million jobs in 1973 to 4.8 million by 1982, a gain of 1.7 million. Manufacturing employment decreased by 1.3 million jobs during this same period.

Chapter Seven

RACIAL AND ETHNIC INCOME VARIATIONS

The relationship of race/ethnicity and income in the United States has long been the target of substantial attention. While this has included concern about native Americans and, increasingly, persons of Spanish origin, primary focus has centered on black-white income variations. The purpose of this chapter is to continue the examination of the distributional patterns of income, detailing particularly black-white and Spanish origin-white income differentials across the range of family configurations. Greater precision is available for the black analysis due to the more comprehensive (yet still historically inadequate) data that is available for this segment of American society.

THE LONG-TERM BLACK TRAUMA

The complexity of demographic and economic elements in shaping and continuously remolding the avenues for advancement of ethnic groups in America defies easy simplification. The painful economic baseline of American blacks in the decades immediately before the Civil War gripped all but a few isolated pockets: a thin strata of freed blacks in the North together with a small yet surprising number of southern blacks — nominally slaves — but contracting out their services for wages (although subject to paying their ''masters'' a substantial share of their income). The vast majority of blacks were anonymous plantation hands and were to continue as such for most of the century after the Emancipation Proclamation. The momentary post-Civil War euphoria was quickly drowned by the political realities of Reconstruction. The economic submergence that overcame blacks in the skilled trades, if anything, reduced the number of successful aspirants to the middle class. The floodgates of European immigration opened, with a resulting inundation of black skills by white competitors, which dominated the era up to the first World War.

But the substantial limitations placed on overseas migration shortly after World War I were a mainspring for change. In the words of the U.S. President's Research Committee on Social Trends in 1931, " . . . immigration was no sooner restricted than the vacuum thus created drew hundreds of thousands of southern Negroes from the farm to the industrial cities."[1] As late as the Census of 1910, only 4.8 percent of America's southern-born Negroes were living outside that region — and most of these had migrated to the border states of Virginia, Kentucky and Tennessee.[2] The drive to a better life from 1910 to 1920 reflected the pull of opportunities in the North and the push of disorganized agriculture in the South — particularly resulting from boll-weevil infestation. By 1920, 8.1 percent of America's southern-born Negroes lived in the Northeast alone. And this number increased by nearly a million persons between 1920 and 1930.

In 1930, the beginning of the Depression, the portion of America's Negroes who lived in urban areas was fast approaching the equivalent in rural residence (44 to 56 percent), while the decade before the ratio was only one in three. But the vast bulk of rural blacks were still in poverty — tied to staple agriculture which was faltering both for black and white alike. Moreover, urban opportunities, while opening somewhat for blacks in the North, had actually been reduced in the South. Again in the words of *Recent Social Trends*, "The past fifty years . . . have witnessed a gradual incursion of whites to these jobs" [referring to opportunities in the services and manufacturing areas]. "In restaurants serving white patrons, the owners are now usually white rather than Negro, as was common in earlier years. . . . Negro men waiters have been partially displaced by white men or by white or Negro girls."[3] The black-owned barber shop, once predominant, had given way to the European immigrant and entrepreneurs; the building trades, long monopolized by blacks in the South up to and through the Civil War, had become white preserves. Even the Negro locomotive fireman, one of the great protean figures of the post-Civil War America, had been completely replaced by whites. The problems of last in and first out are not new — they characterized the 1920s, with black employment circa 1930 having lost all the gains of the decade.

At this remove of time, it is difficult to remember that the first major New York City department store to employ a black salesperson did not do so until World War II days — the first blacks on the executive training program at Bloomingdale's dated from the mid-1950s. (Neither of the two persons first hired in the latter case survived, and it was a long period before their replacement!)

The dominant black income pattern that resulted from these cross trends

EXHIBIT 1
Median Family Income
Black and Other-White Differential: 1947 to 1982

Year	Total (All Races)	White	Black and Other	Black and Other/ White Ratio
1947	$ 3,031	$ 3,157	$ 1,614	.511
1950	3,319	3,445	1,869	.542
1960	5,620	5,835	3,230	.554
1965	6,957	7,251	3,993	.551
1970	9,867	10,236	6,516	.637
1975	13,719	14,268	9,321	.653
1980	21,023	21,904	13,843	.632
1981	22,388	23,517	14,598	.621
1982	23,433	24,603	15,211	.618

Source: U.S. Bureau of the Census, Current Population Reports, Series P-60, No. 140, *Money Income and Poverty Status of Families and Persons in the United States: 1982 (Advance Data from the March 1983 Current Population Survey)*, U.S. Government Printing Office, Washington, D.C., 1983.

U.S. Bureau of the Census, Current Population Reports, Series P-60, No. 137, *Money Income of Households, Families and Persons in the United States: 1981*, U.S. Government Printing Office, Washington, D.C., 1983; and previous annual editions for the respective years.

clearly was one of extreme modesty. While much should and has been made of an occasional black specialty producer or merchandiser of hair products or southeast insurance near-millionaire, these were notable only in their scarcity. Despite much in the way of fervent rhetoric during the New Deal, the pressures of segregation, demanded by southern political machines and tolerated by their northern counterparts, limited more than token activity. The United States, for example, moved into World War II with a segregated army, and only strong threats by A. Philip Randolph — then the head of the Pullman Car Attendants Union — shifted that pattern. The very fact of limited data availability on black incomes bespeaks the lack of attention paid to them in official circles until the post-World War II generation. Thus, the path toward economic equality on the part of blacks had to move up from a virtual sub-basement level. Even as late as the beginning of World War II, when annual full-time worker money wages for black males are compared to that of all other races, the figures are $639 versus $1,419, with an even greater disproportion for females with an equivalent of $327 versus $863. And these data incorporate only full-time workers — they do not show the im-

EXHIBIT 2
Median Family Income
Black-White Differential: 1970 to 1982
(In Current Dollars)

Year	Total (All Races)	White	Black	Black/White Ratio
1970	$ 9,867	$10,236	$ 6,279	.613
1971	10,285	10,672	6,440	.603
1972	11,116	11,549	6,864	.594
1973	12,051	12,595	7,269	.577
1974	12,902	13,408	8,006	.597
1975	13,719	14,268	8,779	.615
1976	14,958	15,537	9,242	.594
1977	16,009	16,740	9,563	.571
1978	17,640	18,368	10,879	.592
1979	19,661	20,502	11,644	.568
1980	21,023	21,904	12,674	.579
1981	22,388	23,517	13,266	.564
1982	23,433	24,603	13,598	.553

Source: U.S. Bureau of the Census, Current Population Reports, Series P-60, No. 140, *Money Income and Poverty Status of Families and Persons in the United States: 1982 (Advance Data from the March 1983 Current Population Survey)*, U.S. Government Printing Office, Washington, D.C., 1983.

U.S. Bureau of the Census, Current Population Reports, Series P-60, No. 137, *Money Income of Households, Families and Persons in the United States: 1981* U.S. Government Printing Office, Washington, D.C., 1983; and previous annual editions for the respective years.

mense skew in the number and wages of part-time workers in the black community.[4] When the comparative economic position of America's black citizenry is reviewed currently, the unevenness in the starting line must be kept in mind.

THE POST-WORLD WAR II PATTERN

Time-series data on blacks until fairly recently (1970) incorporated them with "other" races. In part, this evidenced the lack of political/economic concern in general and the imbalance in income relationships. It also reflected the relatively small scale of "other" elements. Native Americans did not truly emerge into an element of national economic concern until our own era, while Americans of Spanish origin similarly had not established their own political identity until fairly recently. Thus, in the data earlier cited, as well as that incorporated into Exhibit 1, the median income which is shown distinguishes two groups: "whites," and "black and other."

Unfortunately, when blacks and other races are aggregated, particularly over time, the comparisons blur the harsh realities of the limited, comparative increases in the income of blacks *per se*. The rapid rise, for example, both in number and in affluence, of Oriental-Americans tends to obscure the sharp partitions within this grouping. Nonetheless, this limitation cannot be avoided if we wish to overview the entire post-World War II era.

Despite continuing imbalances, the post-World War II decades were a period of increasing affluence for both of America's major racial groups. Black median family incomes, in current dollars, increased from a little more than $1,600 in 1947 to well over $15,000 by 1982. Whites, on the other hand, started at nearly double the level of median family income in 1947 ($3,157) and swept up to a figure of well over $24,000 by 1982. The ratio of black-and-other median income to that of whites is indicated in the right-hand column of Exhibit 1. From a low of .511 in 1947, the ratio experienced sustained increases through 1975 when it reached .653; the ratio actually peaked in 1978, followed by a distressing downturn in the subsequent four years for which we have data. The ratio for the terminal point of 1982 is .618. Thus, for every thousand dollars of income of white median families, blacks and other families at the midpoint enjoyed only $618. While far better, certainly, than the $511 equivalent of 1947, the relative levels seemingly have returned to those of a decade ago.

The 1970 to 1982 Period

These data, however, cloak very substantial internal variations as a result of such variables as race, age, education, and most importantly, family configuration. It is this last set of elements that has assumed increasing potency over time.

In order to establish an appropriate baseline for demographic linkages, we are fortunate in having consistent data for black-white differentials from 1970-1982. The picture which emerges in Exhibit 2 is far less salubrious than that shown in Exhibit 1. Black incomes in relationship to whites' have declined sharply since 1970 despite intermediate fluctuations. By 1982 the median family incomes for blacks were only 55.3 percent those of whites.

Configurational Variations

In Chapter 5, we stressed the substantial variations in family incomes as a function of demographic configuration. These are particularly striking as we view America's black population. As shown in Exhibit 3, when married-couple families, both white and black, are compared, there are consistently higher gen-

EXHIBIT 3
Median Family Income
Married Couple Families
Total and Wife in Paid Labor Force
Black-White Differentials
(In Current Dollars)

	TOTAL			WIFE IN PAID LABOR FORCE		
Year	**White**	**Black**	**Black/White Ratio**	**White**	**Black**	**Black/White Ratio**
1970	$10,723	$ 7,816	.729	$12,543	$ 9,721	.775
1975	15,125	11,526	.762	17,550	14,355	.818
1976	16,501	13,137	.796	19,046	15,703	.824
1977	17,916	13,716	.766	20,518	17,008	.829
1978	19,368	15,913	.822	22,372	19,073	.853
1979	21,824	16,887	.774	25,313	20,705	.818
1980	23,501	18,593	.791	27,238	22,795	.837
1981	25,474	19,624	.770	29,713	25,040	.843
1982	26,443	20,586	.779	30,801	25,359	.823

Source: U.S. Bureau of the Census, Current Population Reports, Series P-60, No. 140, *Money Income and Poverty Status of Families and Persons in the United States: 1982, (Advance Data from the March 1983 Current Population Survey)*, U.S. Government Printing Office, Washington, D.C. 1983.

U.S. Bureau of the Census, Current Population Reports, Series P-60, No. 137, *Money Income of Households, Families and Persons in the United States: 1981*, U.S. Government Printing Office, Washington, D.C., 1983; and previous annual editions for the respective years.

eral income ratios over time — with black married-couple families in 1982 securing 78 percent of the income of their white peers. This compares to only 55 percent for black families in total versus white families in total.

This is even more forcefully the case when we compare married-couple families with wives in the paid-labor force, as shown in the right-hand side of the exhibit. In 1970, the ratio of black income to white income stood at .775; it has moved up over the eleven years for which data are available to a much more nearly comparable .823 in 1982. Thus, while black families as a whole lost ground to whites from 1970, this did not hold for married-couple families, particularly that subset with wives in the paid labor force. Instead, in this latter category, there was significant progress. By 1982 certainly, black married-couple families by most standards would be viewed as substantially in the middle-class — their median incomes stood slightly above the $20,500 mark. And those married couples with wives in the paid labor force were firmly ensconced with median in-

EXHIBIT 4
Median Family Income
Married Couple Families with Wife Employed Full Time (Total) and with Householder Working Year Round, Full Time, Black-White Differential
(In Current Dollars)

	TOTAL			HOUSEHOLDER YEAR-ROUND, FULL-TIME WORKER		
Year	**White**	**Black**	**Black/White Ratio**	**White**	**Black**	**Black/White Ratio**
1970	N.A.	N.A.	N.A.	N.A.	N.A.	N.A.
1975	$18,530	$15,666	.845	$20,412	$17,874	.876
1976	19,996	17,330	.867	21,641	18,910	.874
1977	21,307	19,112	.897	23,292	20,909	.898
1978	23,498	21,307	.907	25,404	24,465	.963
1979	26,506	23,052	.870	28,450	25,848	.909
1980	28,866	25,352	.878	31,254	28,780	.921
1981	31,565	27,163	.861	34,288	29,876	.871

Source: U.S. Bureau of the Census, Current Population Reports, Series P-60, No. 137, *Money Income of Households, Families and Persons in the United States: 1981*, U.S. Government Printing Office, Washington, D.C., 1983; and previous annual editions for the respective years.

comes over $25,000. By this latter date, white married couples with wives in the paid labor force had incomes just $5,000 higher (under 18 percent) than their black equivalents.

If this path of variation is pursued to yet another partition, married-couple families with wives employed full time, the differential narrows even further. This is shown in the left-hand side of Exhibit 4. While this data series at this writing extended only to 1981, the variation at that time was even less. The median income of black families with wives employed full time ($27,163) in 1981 was 86 percent of their white demographic equivalents ($31,565).

The right-hand side of Exhibit 4 provides data on a further subset: married-couple families with wives employed full time and with householders year-round, full-time workers. It is this group which has made the greatest strides both in absolute increments of income as well as comparative progress. Black median incomes have progressed from a 1975 level of slightly under $18,000 to almost $30,000 by 1981. In this terminal year, their incomes reached 87 percent of their white equivalents.

So striking is the progress within this last group as to be worthy of much greater detailed analysis, certainly more than we can provide within the lim-

EXHIBIT 5
1981 Median Family Income
Married Couple Families, Wife Employed Full Time,
Householder Year-Round, Full-Time Worker
Black-White Differential by Age of Householder
(In Current Dollars)

Age of Householder	White	Black	Black/White Ratio
Total 15 years and over	$34,288	$29,876	.871
15 to 24 years old	22,848	N.A.	—
25 to 34 years old	31,151	28,356	.910
35 to 44 years old	36,107	29,880	.828
45 to 54 years old	39,253	36,796	.937
55 to 64 years old	36,626	29,920	.817
65 years and over	38,110	N.A.	—

Source: U.S. Bureau of the Census, Current Population Reports, Series P-60, No. 137, *Money Income of Households, Families and Persons in the United States: 1981*, U.S. Government Printing Office, Washington, D.C., 1983.

itations of this book. A major question is whether the remaining gap will close over time. Does it perhaps represent merely a time lag? Are older generation incomes disproportionately low resulting from past prejudices and other dated factors, while more youthful individuals are more equivalent? This does not seem to be the case; the relationships shown in Exhibit 5 point to greater equality in the 45 to 54 years age group — the peak earning years.

The downturn in the national economy subsequent to 1979 has wreaked particular havoc on the elite of America's labor force — the heavily unionized blue-collar workers, epitomized in the North Central states by the automobile and steel workers. It is just in this area where black progress has been most striking. In turn, the equivalent degeneration of black incomes is mirrored in Exhibits 3 and 4. At least as of this writing, there is significant question whether there will be a full-scale revitalization — or an equivalently reimbursed replacement set of job openings for America's black population. In any case, the decline in the black/white income ratio in the last several years clearly indicates the challenge faced by the American economy — and society as a whole — in making blacks full economic citizens.

The Single-Spouse Families

Black married-couple families have achieved far greater parity with whites than holds true for single-spouse families, whose incomes are detailed in Exhibit

EXHIBIT 6
Median Family Income
Single Spouse Families
Black-White Differential
(In Current Dollars)

	MALE HOUSEHOLDER			FEMALE HOUSEHOLDER		
Year	**White**	**Black**	**Black/White Ratio**	**White**	**Black**	**Black/White Ratio**
1970	$ 9,524	$ 6,751	.709	$ 5,754	$3,576	.621
1975	13,793	8,955	.649	7,651	4,898	.640
1976	13,530	10,277	.760	8,226	5,069	.616
1977	15,630	10,296	.659	8,799	5,598	.636
1978	16,914	12,080	.714	9,911	5,888	.594
1979	17,700	12,491	.706	11,452	6,906	.603
1980	18,731	12,557	.670	11,908	7,425	.624
1981	20,421	14,489	.710	12,508	7,506	.600
1982	21,416	14,661	.685	13,496	7,458	.553

Source: U.S. Bureau of the Census, Current Population Reports, Series P-60, No. 140, *Money Income and Poverty Status of Families and Persons in the United States: 1982 (Advance Data from the March 198 3 Current Population Survey)*, U.S. Government Printing Office, Washington, D.C., 1983.

U.S. Bureau of the Census, Current Population Reports, Series P-60, No. 137, *Money Income of Households, Families and Persons in the United States: 1981*, U.S. Government Printing Office, Washington, D.C., 1983; and previous annual editions for the respective years.

6. Not only are absolute incomes relatively low, but in general the black-white differential is substantial. Male householder median incomes among whites had moved from $9,500 in 1970 to a level just in excess of $21,000 by 1982. Black male householder median incomes made no relative progress in the same period of time, moving from a base of $6,751 in 1970 to just under $15,000 by 1982 — a nearly constant ratio over time of about 70 percent.

The family-income figures for female householders are even more striking. In the absolute, for both whites and blacks, they are abysmally low. The median income of white female householders stood at $5,574 in 1970, and moved up to slightly below the $13,500 mark by 1982. The latter, however, was just slightly more than half of the median family income for all white families. While the white parameter is modest at best, the black equivalent is truly tragic. In 1970, the black female householder median income — $3,576 — was 62 percent of that of whites; by 1982, the median family income of black female householders — $7,458 — had declined to only 55 percent that of their white counterparts, and

EXHIBIT 7
Black/White Median Family Income Ratios, by Family Type and Employment Status: 1970 to 1982

		Married Couple Families					
			Wife in Paid Labor Force				
				Wife Employed Full Time			
Year	Total	Total	Total	Total	Householder Year-Round Full-Time Worker	Male House-holder	Female house-holder
1970	.613	.729	.775	N.A.	N.A.	.709	.621
1975	.615	.762	.818	.845	.876	.649	.640
1976	.594	.796	.824	.867	.874	.760	.616
1977	.571	.766	.829	.897	.898	.659	.636
1978	.592	.822	.853	.907	.963	.714	.594
1979	.568	.774	.818	.870	.909	.706	.603
1980	.579	.791	.837	.878	.921	.670	.624
1981	.562	.770	.843	.861	.871	.710	.600
1982	.553	.779	.823	—	—	.685	.553

Source: U.S. Bureau of the Census, Current Population Reports, Series P-60, No. 140, *Money Income and Poverty Status of Families and Persons in the United States: 1982 (Advance Data from the March 1983 Current Population Survey)*, U.S. Government Printing Office, Washington, D.C., 1983.

U.S. Bureau of the Census, Current Population Reports, Series P-60, No. 137, *Money Income of Households, Families and Persons in the United States: 1981*, U.S. Government Printing Office, Washington, D.C., 1983; and previous annual editions for the respective years.

EXHIBIT 8
Changing Black-White Family Composition: 1975 to 1982
(Numbers in Thousands)
(Families as of March of the following year)

	1975		1982		Change: 1975 to 1982	
	Number	Percent	Number	Percent	Number	Percent
White						
All Families	49,873	100.0	53,407	100.0	3,534	7.1
Married Couple Families	43,311	86.8	45,252	84.7	1,941	4.5
Wife in Paid Labor Force	18,609	37.3	22,692	42.5	4,083	21.9
Wife Not in Paid Labor Force	24,702	49.5	22,560	42.2	−2,142	−8.7
Male Householder, Spouse Absent	1,182	2.4	1,648	3.1	466	39.4
Female Householder, Spouse Absent	5,380	10.8	6,507	12.2	1,127	20.9
Black						
All Families	5,586	100.0	6,503	100.0	944	16.9
Married Couple Families	3,352	60.0	3,486	53.4	134	4.0
Wife in Paid Labor Force	1,903	34.1	2,115	32.4	212	11.1
Wife Not in Paid Labor Force	1,449	25.9	1,372	21.0	− 77	−5.3
Male Householder, Spouse Absent	230	4.1	309	4.7	79	34.3
Female Householder, Spouse Absent	2,004	35.9	2,734	41.9	730	36.4

Source: U.S. Bureau of the Census, Current Population Reports, Series P-60, No. 140, *Money Income and Poverty Status of Families and Persons in the United States: 1982 (Advance Data from the March 1983 Current Population Survey)*, U.S. Government Printing Office, Washington, D.C., 1983.

U.S. Bureau of the Census, Current Population Reports, Series P-60, No. 137, *Money Income of Households, Families and Persons in the United States: 1981*, U.S. Government Printing Office, Washington, D.C., 1983; and previous annual editions for the respective years.

thus the income level for black female householders, paltry at best, actually is shrinking as a proportion of all equivalent household incomes.

In order to provide a summary documentation of the linkage between family configuration and black-white income differentials, the data in Exhibit 7 provide a synopsis of the material presented. As is evident, the lowest ratio (i.e., the largest differential) of black-to-white income is for total families: it moves up (i.e., the gap narrows) in a smooth pattern from married-couple households to those with wives in the paid labor force, to those with wives employed full time, to its high, wives employed full time and with householders year-round, full-time workers. A substantial part of the income variance between blacks and whites, therefore, is a function of the relative frequency of single-spouse families.

It is the variation in family composition between blacks and whites which particularly accentuates the statistical comparison of median family incomes (Exhibit 8). In 1975, for example, barely one in eight white families were male or female householders with spouses absent. The equivalent for blacks, however, was four in ten.

This was the highest-growth family configuration for both whites and blacks in the period up through 1982. By this latter year, one in six whites (15.3 percent) were male or female households with spouse absent. The proportion among blacks, however, had moved up to the 46.6 percent mark. Over four in ten of *all* black families by 1982 comprised female householders (spouse absent) — the lowest of all income groups, and the group whose income ratio to its white equivalent has been least salubrious.

By 1982, more than four in ten (42.5 percent) of all white families had wives in the paid labor force — the highest income category isolated in Exhibit 8. The equivalent for blacks was only one in three (32.4 percent), although among married-couple families, blacks have proportionately more wives in the labor force. The single largest black family type are female householders.

Symptom and independent factor can often be mistaken for one another. The data presented here indicate a very strong relationship between both absolute and comparative income levels and family configuration. In turn, however, family configuration may be a result of employment availability and consistency. At the very least it reflects unemployment rates most directly, as well as a whole host of other factors, to say nothing of history. While the income progress made by married-couple configurations — particularly the "two-worker" subset — is most heartening, the other side of the coin is the more rapidly increasing dominance — and comparative impoverishment — of black female householders.

SPANISH ORIGIN

The formalization of data by government — and equally significantly, the lack

EXHIBIT 9
Median Family Income
White-Spanish Origin Differential
1972 to 1982
(In Current Dollars)

Year	White	Spanish Origin of Householder	Spanish Origin/ White Origin
1972	$11,549	$ 8,188	.709
1975	14,268	9,551	.669
1976	15,537	10,259	.660
1977	16,740	11,421	.682
1978	18,368	12,566	.684
1979	20,502	14,569	.711
1980	21,904	14,717	.672
1981	23,517	16,402	.697
1982	24,603	16,227	.660

Source: U.S. Bureau of the Census, Current Population Reports, Series P-60, No. 140, *Money Income and Poverty Status of Families and Persons in the United States: 1982 (Advance Data from the March 1983 Current Population Survey)*, U.S. Government Printing Office, Washington, D.C., 1983.

U.S. Bureau of the Census, Current Population Reports, Series P-60, No. 137, *Money Income of Households, Families and Persons in the United States: 1981*, U.S. Government Printing Office, Washington, D.C., 1983; and previous annual editions for the respective years.

thereof — gives some insight into the dimensions of self-consciousness, coherency, and ultimately the direction of political clout within our society. Within that context, it is striking to note that it was not until 1972 that the Current Population Survey singled out those of Spanish origin and provided continuous and ongoing data for this important sector of American society. Their pattern of overall median family income compared with that of whites is shown in Exhibit 9. In 1982, basically for every thousand dollars of family income of white median families, those of Spanish origin had roughly $660. There was relatively little variation in this unequal relationship during the period shown in Exhibit 9.

The ratio of Spanish origin median family incomes to those of whites is substantially higher than holds true for blacks (Exhibit 2). In 1982, for example, the Spanish origin-white ratio was 66 percent; for the black-to-white equivalent it was barely 56 percent. While in the latter case the gap has widened over time, as indicated earlier, the relationship for those of Spanish origin has remained somewhat more stable.

EXHIBIT 10
Spanish Origin/White Median Family Income Ratios, by Family Type And Employment Status: 1975 to 1981

		MARRIED COUPLE FAMILIES				
			Wife in Labor Force			
Year	Total	Total	Total	Householder Year-Round Full-Time Worker	Male House-holder	Female House-holder
1975	.669	.722	.788	.812	.755	.625
1977	.682	.729	.785	.809	.808	.621
1978	.684	.760	.800	.808	.712	.563
1979	.711	.771	.810	.832	.822	.580
1980	.672	.739	.795	.808	.710	.590
1981	.697	.759	.796	.808	.724	.606
1982	.660	.731	.795	.813	.806	.551

Source: U.S. Bureau of the Census, Current Population Reports, Series P-60, No. 140, *Money Income and Poverty Status of Families and Persons in the United States: 1982 (Advance Data from the March 1983 Current Population Survey)*, U.S. Government Printing Office, Washington, D.C., 1983.

U.S. Bureau of the Census, Current Population Reports, Series P-60, No. 137, *Money Income of Households, Families and Persons in the United States: 1981*, U.S. Government Printing Office, Washington, D.C., 1983; and previous annual editions for the respective years.

Again, however, the all-inclusive family data mask internal variations of substance. These are shown in Exhibit 10 which provides the ratios of median family incomes for those of Spanish origin to all white family incomes by a limited number of family types. (It should be noted that the partitions of Exhibit 10 are not fully comparable to Exhibit 7 in terms of married-couple families, wife in paid labor force versus wife employed full time. These latter data are not available for those of Spanish origin.)

Again it is striking to note that as we move from total families first to married-couple families as a whole, and then to those families with wives in the paid labor force, the relationship to equivalent white median family incomes rises substantially. When those with wives in the paid labor force and with the householder a year-round full-time worker are considered, the ratio moves past the 80 percent mark.

Yet for most demographic sectors within the married couple set, those of Spanish origin fall below their black equivalent (see Exhibit 7). However, as we

EXHIBIT 11
Changing Spanish Origin Family Composition: 1975 to 1982
(Numbers in Thousands)
(Families as of March of the following year)

	1975		1982		Change: 1975 to 1982	
Family Configuration	**Number**	**Percent**	**Number**	**Percent**	**Number**	**Percent**
All Families	2,499	100.0	3,369	100.0	870	34.8
Married Couple Families	1,896	75.9	2,448	72.7	552	29.1
Wife in Paid Labor Force	790	31.6	1,123	33.3	333	42.2
Wife Not in Paid Labor Force	1,107	44.3	1,325	39.3	218	19.6
Male Householder (Spouse Absent)	82	3.3	153	4.5	71	86.6
Female Householder (Spouse Absent)	522	20.9	767	22.8	245	46.9

Source: U.S. Bureau of the Census, Current Population Reports, Series P-60, No. 140, *Money Income and Poverty Status of Families and Persons in the United States: 1982 (Advance Data from the March 1983 Current Population Survey)*, U.S. Government Printing Office, Washington, D.C., 1983.

U.S. Bureau of the Census, Current Population Reports, Series P-60, No. 137, *Money Income of Households, Families and Persons in the United States: 1981*. U.S. Government Printing Office, Washington, D.C., 1983; and previous annual editions for the respective years.

have noted, when all families are considered, their median income is higher. The incongruity is accounted by the rival incidence of male and female householders. The key is the incidence rates of these predominantly lower-level income groupings. Among those of Spanish origin, male and female householders (with spouse absent) accounted for 27.3 percent of all families (Exhibit 11) in 1982. While this represents a substantial increase from 24.2 percent in 1975, the single spouse incidence was strikingly lower than that of blacks, where more than four in ten were non-married couple families. In both cases, those of Spanish origin have slightly higher incomes than holds true for blacks.

Thus, while income levels among married-couple families of Spanish origin are actually more modest than their black counterparts, the lower incidence rate of single-spouse families means that all Spanish-origin families as a group have median incomes in excess of that of blacks. When compared, however, with total whites as a group, the situation is far less salubrious, with median income levels roughly two-thirds those of the former.

SUMMARY

Reflecting the volatile economic swings of the 1970s, as well as the recessionary trauma of the early 1980s, the incomes of blacks and Spanish-origin Americans have faltered.

1. Black incomes in 1970 were 61.3 percent of white incomes. By 1982, despite intraperiod fluctuations, the black-white income ratio declined to 55.3 percent.
2. There are, however, substantial income variations across the major demographic partitions. In 1982, the median income of black married-couple families was 77.9 percent that of their white equivalents. The median income of black married-couple families with wives in the paid labor force was 82.3 percent of their white peers. When both spouses of the latter subset are employed full time, the black-white income ratio approaches 90 percent (1981). Generally, these ratios have improved over the last 12 years.
3. More than counterbalancing the relative improvement of these demographic sectors has been the relative income deterioration of female householder (single-spouse) families. The black-white income ratio has fallen from 62.1 percent in 1970 to 55.3 percent in 1982. It is the variation in family composition between blacks and whites which particularly accentuates the statistical comparison of median family incomes.
4. By 1982, over four in ten of all black families comprised female householders (spouse absent), the lowest of all the income groups, the fastest growing household type, and the group whose income ratio to its white equivalent has been least salubrious.

5. The ratio of Spanish origin median family incomes to those of whites is substantially higher than holds true for blacks. In 1982, for example, the Spanish origin-white ratio was 66 percent; the black-to-white ratio was barely 55 percent. While in the latter case the gap has widened over time, the relationship for those of Spanish origin has remained somewhat more stable.
6. Again, as we move from total families to married-couple families as a whole, and then to those families with wives in the paid labor force, the relationship to equivalent white median family incomes rises substantially. When those with wives in the paid labor force and with the householder a year-round full-time worker are considered, the ratio moves past the 80 percent mark.

NOTES

1. Report of the President's Research Committee on Social Trends, *Recent Social Trends in the United States* (New York: McGraw-Hill, 1933), p. 555.
2. *Ibid*. p. 566.
3. *Ibid*.
4. U.S. Bureau of the Census, *Historical Statistics of the United States, Colonial Times to 1970 - Part 2* (Washington, D.C.: U.S. Government Printing Office, 1976). p. 305.

Chapter Eight

POVERTY

Who is in the caboose of the American economic/demographic train? What are the baseline trends? While some reference was made in the previous chapter to the linkage between low-income levels and household configurations, the issues of poverty are so potent within our society as to be worthy of a fuller description.

There is no monolithic standard for poverty. The vagaries of lifestyle, of region, of definition as to what is an adequate threshold level of income — to say nothing of the issues of what is to be counted as income — have all made this a most complex topic. The most commonly accepted definition in the United States, however, and the one which is used in the chapter which follows, is that generated by the U.S. Bureau of the Census and detailed in Exhibit 1.

While this does not include the noncash elements of support — such as food stamps, Medicaid and public housing which have grown very substantially since the era of the Great Society — it does provide a useful series of threshold points.[1] It further has the advantage of having been updated over time — thus keeping a reasonably consistent market basket of necessities free from the distortions of inflation.

THE SCALE OF THE PHENOMENON

The pattern of persons below the poverty level from 1960 through 1982 — the last date for which data are available at this writing — is shown in Exhibit 2. The long period of relative economic stagnation in the latter 1950s, now viewed by some observers with nostalgia, left a baseline level in 1960 of nearly 40 million Americans below the poverty level, or more than one in five (22.2 percent) of all

EXHIBIT 1
Weighted Average Poverty Thresholds in 1982

Size of Family Unit	Threshold
1 person (unrelated individual)	$ 4,901
15 to 64 years	5,019
65 years and over	4,626
2 persons	6,281
Householder 15 to 64 years	6,487
Householder 65 years and over	5,836
3 persons	7,693
4 persons	9,862
5 persons	11,684
6 persons	13,207
7 persons	15,036
8 persons	16,719
9 persons or more	19,698

Source: U.S. Bureau of the Census, Current Population Reports, Series P-60, No. 140, *Money Income and Poverty Status of Families and Persons in the United States: 1982. (Advance Data from the March 1983 Current Population Survey)*, U.S. Government Printing Office, Washington, D.C., 1983.

Definition: Families and unrelated individuals are classified as being above or below the poverty level using the poverty index originated at the Socal Security Administration in 1964 and revised by Federal Interagency Committees in 1969 and 1980. The poverty index is based solely on money income and does not reflect the fact that many low-income persons receive noncash benefits such as food stamps, Medicaid, and public housing. The index is based on the Department of Agriculture's 1961 Economy Food Plan and reflects the different consumption requirements of families based on their size and composition. It was determined from the Department of Agriculture's 1955 Survey of Food Consumption that families of three or more persons spend approximately one-third of their income on food; the poverty level for these families was, therefore, set at three times the cost of the Economy Food Plan. For smaller families and persons living alone, the cost of the Economy Food Plan was multiplied by factors that were slightly higher in order to compensate for the relatively larger fixed expenses of these smaller households. The poverty thresholds are updated every year to reflect changes in the Consumer Price Index (CPI). The average poverty threshold for a family of four was $9,862 in 1982, about 6.1 percent higher than the comparable 1981 cutoff of $9,287. Weighted average poverty thresholds by size of family are shown above.

EXHIBIT 2
Persons Below the Poverty Level, Total and 65 Years of Age and Over: 1960 to 1982
(Numbers in Thousands)

	Total		Poverty Rate %	
	All Persons	**65 Years and Over**	**All Persons**	**65 Years and Over**
1960	39,851	5,481*	22.2	35.2*
1970	25,420	4,709	12.5	24.5
1973	22,973	3,354	11.1	16.3
1980	29,272	3,871	13.0	15.7
1981	31,822	3,853	14.0	15.3
1982	34,398	3,751	15.0	14.6

Intraperiod Changes

	Number	Percent
Total Persons		
1960-1973†	−16,878	−42.4
1973-1982	11,425	49.7
65 Years and Over		
1960-1973†	−2,172	−38.8
1973-1982	397	11.8

*1959 data.
†1959 to 1973 data for 65 years of age and over.

Source: U.S. Bureau of the Census, Current Population Reports, Series P-60, No. 140, *Money Income and Poverty Status of Families and Persons in the United States: 1982. (Advance Data from the March 1983 Current Population Survey)*, U.S. Government Printing Office, Washington, D.C., 1983.

Americans at that time. The situation was even more striking among persons sixty-five years of age and over — with more than one in three (35.2 percent) holding this sad status. While the latter group has shrunk substantially over time — in large measure a tribute to the potency of Social Security boosts and later indexation — even as late as 1982, one in seven Americans over the age of sixty-five years was below the poverty level.

For the nation as a whole, however, the pattern was somewhat different. While

EXHIBIT 3
Persons Below the Poverty Level, White, Black and Spanish Origin: 1960 to 1982
(Numbers in Thousands)

	White	Black	Spanish Origin
1960	28,309	9,927*	N.A.
1970	17,484	7,548	N.A.
1973	15,142	7,388	2,366
1980	19,699	8,579	3,491
1981	21,553	9,173	3,713
1982	23,517	9,697	4,301

Intraperiod Changes

	Number	Percent
White		
1960-1973	−13,167	−46.5
1973-1982	8,375	55.3
Black		
1960-1973†	−2,539	−25.6
1973-1982	2,309	31.3
Spanish Origin		
1960-1973	N.A.	N.A.
1973-1982	1,935	81.8

*1959
†1959 to 1973

Source: U.S. Bureau of the Census, Current Population Reports, Series P-60, No. 140, *Money Income and Poverty Status of Families and Persons in the United States: 1982. (Advance Data from the March 1983 Current Population Survey)*, U.S. Government Printing Office, Washington, D.C., 1983.

there was an abrupt decline from 1960 to 1973 from nearly 40 million persons to barely half that number — 22.9 million — the economic reversals of the latter 1970s are mirrored in the expansion to nearly 30 million persons by 1980. In the last two years alone, there has been an additional increase of more than 5 million persons in poverty. By 1982, the poverty rate for all persons — which had been driven down to the 11.1 percent mark in 1973 — had risen to 15 percent. (The intraperiod changes are shown at the bottom of the exhibit.)

The improvements from 1960 to 1973 were almost wiped out by 1982. The general real income level stagnation of the period (see Chapter 5) severely im-

EXHIBIT 4
Poverty Rates, White, Black and Spanish Origin: 1960 to 1982

	White	Black	Spanish Origin
1960	17.8%	55.1%*	N.A.
1970	9.9	33.5	N.A.
1973	8.4	31.4	21.9
1980	10.2	32.5	25.7
1981	11.1	34.2	26.5
1982	12.0	35.6	29.9
Percent Change			
1960-1973	−52.8	−43.0†	N.A.
1973-1982	42.8	13.4	36.5

*1959
†1959 to 1973

Source: U.S. Bureau of the Census, Current Population Reports, Series P-60, No. 140, *Money Income and Poverty Status of Families and Persons in the United States: 1982. (Advance Data from the March 1983 Current Population Survey),* U.S. Government Printing Office, Washington, D.C., 1983.

pacted the lower end of the economic spectrum. In contrast to this is the much more salubrious situation as we turn to persons sixty-five years and over. But even here, once again, the number of such individuals below the poverty rate is roughly equal to the population of Norway, and indeed the all-person total is two-thirds the size of the total population of France. These are far from trivial numbers and are very basic to the ongoing economic debate which dominates our time: are these individuals who are so far removed from the basic economy as to be relatively untouched by general economic growth, requiring unique and specific subsidy mechanisms and support structures in order to be integrated into the overall society? Or rather, does the philosophy espoused a score of years ago by then-President Kennedy — that a rising tide floats all boats — still hold as it did in the 1960s? While resolution of this issue is well beyond our competence — some of the demographic linkages do illustrate the ramifications.

POVERTY: RACE AND ETHNICITY

Poverty in America is strongly linked to race and ethnicity. As shown in Exhibit 3, when 1960 is compared directly to 1982, poverty among whites declined by some 5 million persons, while it was practically static among blacks.

EXHIBIT 5
Poverty Rates, in Percent, by Family Status of Persons White, Black and Spanish Origin: 1960 to 1982

		IN FAMILIES		
	Total	Total	Householder	Related Children Under 18
White				
1960	17.8	16.2	14.9	20.0
1973	8.4	6.9	6.6	9.7
1982	12.0	10.6	9.6	16.5
Black				
1960*	55.1	54.9	48.1	65.6
1973	31.4	30.8	28.1	40.6
1982	35.6	34.9	33.0	47.3
Spanish Origin				
1960	N.A.	N.A.	N.A.	N.A.
1973	21.9	21.5	19.8	27.8
1982	29.9	29.2	27.2	38.9

*1959 data

Source: U.S. Bureau of the Census, Current Population Reports, Series P-60, No. 140, *Money Income and Poverty Status of Families and Persons in the United States: 1982. (Advance Data from the March 198 3 Current Population Survey)*, U.S. Government Printing Office, Washington, D.C., 1983.

While the time-series for persons of Spanish origin is more limited, the increment in the poverty level — though linked in part to their increase in total numbers — shows a decidedly upward shift since 1973. It is interesting to note, however, that the stagflation of the latter 1970s has impacted whites — at least gauged by 1973 to 1982 growth rates in the number of persons below the poverty level — more than blacks, with the respective increments at 55.3 percent versus 31.3 percent. (The intraperiod changes are detailed at the bottom of Exhibit 3.)

The absolute poverty rates, however, as shown in Exhibit 4, still indicate the racial skew. While fewer than one in eight (12.0 percent) of America's whites was below the poverty level in 1982, the same held true for more than one in three blacks (35.6 percent), and three out of ten persons (29.9 percent) of Spanish origin. The progress made in the era of the 1960s, marked by powerful economic growth which permitted a near halving of white poverty rates — and a

EXHIBIT 6
Poverty Rates in Percent, Persons in Families with Female Householder (No Husband Present): 1960 to 1983

	Total	Householder	Related Children Under 18
White			
1960	39.0	34.0	59.9
1973	28.0	24.5	42.1
1982	30.9	27.9	46.6
Black			
1960*	70.6	65.4	81.6
1973	56.5	52.7	67.2
1982	58.8	56.2	70.7
Spanish Origin			
1960	N.A.	N.A.	N.A.
1973	57.4	51.4	68.7
1982	60.1	55.4	71.8

*1959 data

Source: U.S. Bureau of the Census, Current Population Reports, Series P-60, No. 140, *Money Income and Poverty Status of Families and Persons in the United States: 1982. (Advance Data from the March 1983 Current Population Survey)*, U.S. Government Printing Office, Washington, D.C., 1983.

decline in black poverty rates of over 40 percent — has largely been vitiated. This paralleled the downturn of the economy which has characterized the years since 1973. The real income gains earlier described from 1960 to 1973 (see Chapter 5) gave way to the stagflation of the post-1973 era — with real median family incomes diminishing. The poverty rates clearly reflect this phenomenon. Thus, a strong growth in the economy may not float all boats — but to paraphrase the familiar platitude, it certainly floats a fair number of them.

FAMILY STATUS AND POVERTY RATES

Poverty is not a respecter of family status. It has an even greater incidence among children than it does among adults. Thus, as shown in Exhibit 5, while slightly more than one in ten (10.6 percent) white persons in families were under the poverty level in 1982, the same held true for no less than one in six (16.5 percent) related children under the age of eighteen. This situation was even more

EXHIBIT 7
Families Below the Poverty Level, Total, White, Black and Spanish Origin: 1982

		Below Poverty Level	
	Total	**Number**	**Percent**
Total			
All Families	61,393	7,512	12.2
Families with Female Householder*	9,469	3,434	36.3
(Percent of Total)	(15.4%)	(45.7%)	—
White			
All Families	53,407	5,118	9.6
Families with Female Householder*	6,507	1,813	27.9
(Percent of Total)	(12.2%)	(35.4%)	—
Black			
All Families	6,530	2,158	33.0
Families with Female Householder*	2,734	1,535	56.2
(Percent of Total)	(41.9%)	(71.1%)	—
Spanish Origin			
All Families	3,369	916	27.2
Families with Female Householder*	767	425	55.4
(Percent of Total)	(22.8%)	(46.4%)	—

*No Husband Present (Spouse Absent)

Source: U.S. Bureau of the Census, Current Population Reports, Series P-60, No. 140, *Money Income and Poverty Status of Families and Persons in the United States: 1982. (Advance Data from the March 1983 Current Population Survey)*, U.S. Government Printing Office, Washington, D.C., 1983.

horrendous among black Americans, with slightly more than one in three (34.9 percent) persons in families under the poverty level — but nearly half (47.3 percent) of all children in similar households. The Spanish-origin group in 1982 stood intermediate at 29.2 percent and 38.9 percent, respectively.

THE LINKAGE TO FEMALE HOUSEHOLDERS

The powerful linkage of poverty status and female householders (spouse absent) is brought forward in Exhibit 6. As discussed in the previous chapter, this family configuration has had the fastest growth rate of all types in America — and it is these very families which tend to be linked most intimately to poverty status. For both black and Spanish-origin Americans, almost six out of ten persons in female householder families in 1982 were below the poverty level. This phenomenon is terrifyingly evident as we turn to related children under the age of eighteen in female-householder families: here, both for black and Spanish groups alike, the proportion of children under the poverty level was more than seven in ten in 1982. While the white equivalent — at 46.5 percent — clearly is much lower, it still represents nearly half of the total number of children in families with female householders (no husband present).

As the linkage of age and poverty has been reduced, the importance of the role of the female householder (spouse absent) in poverty statistics has become ever more evident. Again, as earlier discussed, the issue of whether, given a stronger economic base and more jobs for the relatively unskilled, there would be a stronger familial base which would keep men within the family, must be kept in mind. Regardless, however, of the antecedents of the problem, the statistical results are all too clear — they are pictured in Exhibit 7.

Nearly 9.5 million of America's 61.4 million families as of 1982 had female householders — or 15.4 percent. But while families below the poverty level as a whole numbered 7.5 million (12.2 percent), among female-householder families it was fully 3.4 million — 36.3 percent of this group. Thus, more than four in ten of all families under the poverty level had female householders, or some 45.7 percent of all poverty families.

The situation is even more striking among blacks. More than seven in ten (71.1 percent) of all black families below the poverty level had female householders. Indeed, well more than half — 56.2 percent — of all black families with a female householder were below the poverty level. It is striking to note that if non-female householder black families are isolated, less than one in five is below the poverty level.

Female householders are much less prevalent among persons of Spanish origin, but even there, more than half — 55.4 percent — are below the poverty level.

Cause and effect in the absolute are beyond our canon. A strong economy, though it may not be a sufficient condition to completely eliminate poverty, clearly is a most important and essential one. It is only with this stipulation that income growth, to say nothing of adequate transfer payments for those incapable of joining the labor force, can be provided.

SUMMARY

The growth in poverty in the United States after the first oil shock of 1973 has been substantial. Its growth was also given impetus by the demographic trends of the past ten years.

1. The number of persons below the poverty level declined by nearly half from 1960 to 1973, from 39.9 million to 23.0 million. By 1982, the trough of the last recession, the poverty level population increased to 34.4 million people.
2. The overall (all persons) poverty rate increased from 11.1 percent in 1973 to 15.0 percent by 1982. During the same time span, the poverty rate for those 65 years and older fell from 16.3 percent to 14.6 percent, a level in 1982 below that for the overall population.
3. Poverty in America is strongly linked to race and ethnicity. In 1982, the white rate stood at 12.0 percent, far below that of blacks (35.6 percent), or the Spanish-origin rate (29.9 percent). However, the growth in the white poverty rate between 1973 and 1982 was far higher than that of the other two groups.
4. Poverty is also linked to family status. For both black and Spanish-origin Americans, almost six out of ten persons in female-householder (single spouse) families in 1982 were below the poverty level. More than four in ten of *all* families under the poverty level had female householders (single spouse), or some 45.7 percent of all poverty families.

NOTE

1. When the monetary value of noncash benefits are estimated and included as income, the Census Bureau indicates that the number of poor would be reduced by between 12 and 42 percent from the current money income poverty definition. See: U.S. Bureau of the Census, Technical Paper No. 50, *Alternative Methods for Valuing Selected In-Kind Transfer Benefits and Measuring Their Effect on Poverty*, U.S. Government Printing Office, Washington, D.C., 1982. See also: U.S. Bureau of the Census, Current Population Reports, Series P-60, No. 136, *Characteristics of Households and Persons Receiving Selected Noncash Benefits: 1981*, U.S. Government Printing Office, Washington, D.C., 1983.

Appendix A

GNP, PERSONAL INCOME AND DISPOSABLE PERSONAL INCOME

The purpose of the Appendix is to briefly highlight the relationship of personal income to GNP within the national income and product accounts, review the shifting composition of personal income, and introduce another gauge of the public's economic wherewithal — disposable personal income.

RELATION OF GNP AND PERSONAL INCOME

Exhibit A-1 provides a partial overview of the national income and product accounts, a summation reflecting the entire complex of the nation's economic income and output and the interaction of its major components. As detailed for 1981, the gross national product (GNP) of the United States — the total national output of goods and services valued at market prices — stood just above $2.9 trillion. Net national product is derived from GNP after taking into account allowances for depreciation of fixed business capital (capital consumption allowances); in 1981 the net national product totalled $2.6 trillion.

Net national income, the next major item in the accounts, reveals aggregate labor and property earnings arising in the current production of goods and services by the nation's economy. Thus it measures the total factor costs of the goods and services produced by the economy; it is roughly equivalent to net national product minus indirect business taxes (such as sales and excise taxes). Totaling $2.35 trillion, net national income mainly differs from GNP in terms of depreciation and indirect business taxes.

The relationship of personal income to net national income is also detailed in

EXHIBIT A-1
Relation of GNP, National Income and Personal Income: 1981
(In Billions of Dollars)

Gross National Product			*$2,937.7*
	Less:	Capital Consumption Allowances	330.1
Equals: *Net National Product*			*2,607.9*
	Plus:	Subsidies Less Current Surplus of Government Enterprises	6.6
	Less:	Indirect Business Tax on Nontax Liability	251.3
	:	Business Transfer Payments	12.4
	:	Statistical Discrepancy	–1.9
Equals: *Net National Income*			*2,352.5*
	Less:	Corporate Profits	190.6
	:	Net Interest	235.7
	:	Contributions for Social Insurance	238.1
	Plus:	Government Transfer Payments to Persons	323.9
	:	Personal Interest Income	329.0
	:	Personal Dividend Income	62.5
	:	Business Transfer Payments	12.4
Equals: *Personal Income*			*2,415.8*

Source: Survey of Current Business, Volume 62, Number 7, July 1982.

Exhibit 1. After corporate profits, net interest and contributions for social insurance are deleted from net national income, and government transfer payments (largely to persons retired, on welfare or out of work), personal interest and dividend income, and business transfer payments are added, personal income is established. The latter totalled $2.4 trillion in 1981, over $60 billion greater than net national income. This is a consequence of the magnitude of government transfer payments.

COMPOSITION OF PERSONAL INCOME

Exhibit A-2 details the major components of personal income and their shifts over time. The major growth sectors include personal interest income (from 6.2 percent of personal income in 1960 to 13.6 percent in 1981) and government transfer payments (from 7.2 percent to 13.9 percent between 1960 and 1981). The former was the consequence of higher interest rates, reflecting inflation, and

EXHIBIT A-2
Personal Income and its Disposition
(In Billions of Current Dollars)

	1960	1973	1981	1960	1973	1981
Total	$402	$1,065	$2,416	100.0%	100.0%	100.0%
Wage and Salary Disbursements	272	703	1,494	67.7	66.0	61.8
Other Labor Income	11	49	140	2.7	4.6	5.8
Proprietors' Income	47	94	125	11.7	8.8	5.2
Rental Income of Persons	14	23	34	3.5	2.2	1.4
Dividends	13	27	63	3.2	2.5	2.6
Personal Interest Income	25	94	329	6.2	8.8	13.6
Transfer Payments	29	120	336	7.2	11.3	13.9
Social Insurance Contribution	-9	-43	-105	-2.2	-4.0	-4.3

Source: *Survey of Current Business*, Volume 62, Number 7, July 1982.

their ancillary — major changes in financial institutions such as the growth of money market funds and financial deregulation. The latter is a result of the general expansion of transfer payments in the 1970s, their indexing (increasing benefit levels as a direct function of inflation), and to their specific behavior in 1980-81, i.e., transfer payments tend to expand during recessionary periods.

The swelling of these two categories of income has tended to lessen the relative importance of wage and salary income, which slipped to 61.8 percent in 1981. Wage and salary income was also adversely affected in 1981 by the recession — many other components of personal income, such as proprietors (the self-employed) and rental income tend to experience relative declines during typical recessions — but it also appears to be experiencing a long-term decline in relative share.

In brief, while personal income in real terms has continued to grow (as detailed in Chapter 3), this has been partially the result of long-term changes in its overall makeup. Bolstering personal income has been the expanding economic role of transfer payments. To the degree the latter is supported by federal deficit spending, it implies that we are borrowing from the future in order to support present income levels.

PERSONAL INCOME AND DISPOSABLE PERSONAL INCOME

Disposable personal income is one of the primary tools of the market analyst.

EXHIBIT A-3
Personal Income and Disposable Personal Income,
U.S. Total: 1960 to 1981
(In Billions of Current Dollars)

Year	Personal Income	Personal Tax and Nontax Payments	Disposable Personal Income
1960	402.3	50.4	352.0
1967	630.0	82.1	547.9
1970	811.1	115.8	695.3
1973	1,065.2	150.7	914.5
1980	2,160.4	336.3	1,824.1
1981	2,415.8	386.7	2,029.1
		Percent Distribution	
1960	100.0	12.5	87.5
1967	100.0	13.0	87.0
1970	100.0	14.3	85.7
1973	100.0	14.1	85.9
1980	100.0	15.6	84.4
1981	100.0	16.0	84.0

Source: *Survey of Current Business*, Volume 62, Number 7, July 1982.

Indeed, many economists consider it to be the best available gauge of the public's buying power and economic wherewithal. It is a measure of the nominal income flow available to potential consumers after making personal tax and nontax payments to various levels of government. The relationship between the several variables at work — of personal income, personal tax and nontax payments, and disposable personal income — for the 1960 to 1981 period is shown in Exhibit A-3. As is evident from the exhibit, nominal personal income grew by six times in the 21-year period. Personal tax and nontax payments, however, exceeded even this rapid rate of growth — with a multiple in 1981 nearly eight times that of the 1960 base. Disposable income, on the other hand — the residual of these two elements — grew by something less than six times, $352 billion in 1960 to slightly in excess of $2 trillion by 1981.

On the bottom of the exhibit, the latter parameters are restated in terms of their share of personal income. Personal tax and nontax payments moved up from 12.5 percent in 1960 — one out of every eight dollars of personal income — to 16 percent in 1981 — or just slightly less than one in six of those same dollars. In turn, disposable income as a percentage of personal income declined from 87.5 percent in 1960 to 84 percent by 1981.

Thus the total personal income — and per capita personal income — measures a somewhat stronger growth trend than disposable personal income. But the differential is not so large as to invalidate the observations presented in Chapter 3, i.e., substitution of disposable personal income for total personal income would not alter the conclusions that were drawn.

INDEX